A Creative Approach to Teaching Writing

The what, why and how of teaching writing in context

by Steve Bowkett

BLOOMSBURY

LONDON · NEW DELHI · NEW YORK · SYDNEY

Bloomsbury Education

An imprint of Bloomsbury Publishing Plc

50 Bedford Square
London
WC1B 3DP
UK

1385 Broadway
New York
NY 10018
USA

www.bloomsbury.com

Bloomsbury is a registered trade mark of Bloomsbury Publishing Plc

First published 2014

British Library Cataloguing-in-Publication Data
A catalogue record for this book is available from the British Library.

ISBN: 978-1-4411-7676-9

Library of Congress Cataloging-in-Publication Data
A catalog record for this book is available from the Library of Congress.

1 3 5 7 9 10 8 6 4 2

Typeset by Newgen Knowledge Works (P) Ltd., Chennai, India
Printed and bound by CPI Group (UK) Ltd, Croydon, CR0 4YY

This book is produced using paper that is made from wood grown in
managed, sustainable forests. It is natural, renewable and recyclable.
The logging and manufacturing processes conform to the environmental
regulations of the country of origin.

To view more of our titles please visit www.bloomsbury.com

Acknowledgements

Many people have helped me over the years to develop as a writer. Most importantly I want to thank the thousands
of children I've met during my visits to schools as a 'real live author', who have almost universally shown the kind of
interest in, enthusiasm for and playfulness with words and stories that lie at the heart of what I have tried to say in
this book.

I am grateful to my friend Tony Hitchman for his generosity in letting me use his artwork. Thanks also to
Melanie Wilson for her encouragement and support for the project at the outset and to her colleagues
Helen Diamond, Holly Gardner and Jane Moses for helping to prepare this book for publication.

I'd like to express my appreciation to the people who took time and trouble to respond to our questionnaire about
their passion for writing. Particular thanks go to author Alan Gibbons who is a Blue Peter award-winning author, has
been shortlisted twice each for the Carnegie Medal and the Booktrust Teenage Prize and has won ten literary awards
for his work. He is the organiser of the Campaign for the Book. Also to Gareth Mottram who is author of the Jason
Willow series of paranormal action novels and, from New Writers UK Julie Malone and Barbara Gidman (www.
newwritersuk.co.uk) and to young writer Bita Yazdani for allowing me to feature some of her work.

Finally I acknowledge the debt I owe to the writer and my friend the late Douglas Hill. We walked the good road
together for a while and he taught me much – I am still learning from him.

Contents

1
Introduction and using this book

'If anyone wishes to write in a clear style, let him be first clear in his thoughts.'
Johann Wolfgang von Goethe (1749–1832) German writer and polymath

An important moment in my development as a writer and as a teacher happened some years ago when I asked my class to write a story: an audible groan went up from a number of the children, but I ignored that. 'Don't worry,' I reassured them. 'I'll help you.' And I wrote the title on the board. Understanding the important principle of 'modelling the behaviour' I had a go at writing too. After about ten minutes one of the boys came over to my table and said 'I can't do this.' 'Well,' I replied cheerfully, 'you just need to think about it.' Then he said what has echoed in my mind ever since: 'But sir, <u>how</u> do I think about it?'

This got me thinking about what I was doing with my imagination that enabled me to write. And, beyond that, could I feed those insights back into my classroom practice to offer the children the 'how to' that perhaps I assumed they already possessed?

I have often since come across the idea that 'you can do anything if you put your mind to it'. That begs the same question – how do you put your mind to it? Trying to find answers has a direct bearing on the appearance of this book and the others in the series. Our aim is to offer practical and effective activities to help empower children with the know-how relevant to their development as writers. Part of the plan for this book has been to gather insights both from professionals in the field and from children themselves who already love writing: these you'll find sprinkled through the chapters together with quotes from traditional sources and authors of classical works.

Our presumption throughout has been that 'enthusiasm is infectious', and that when enjoyment, know-how and opportunity meet the outcomes will be impressive.

Starting to write

Most children can tell you that a story (or indeed any piece of writing) has a beginning, a middle and an end. That's what it looks like when it's finished. Before the writing comes the thinking. Having said this, some authors prefer the 'stream of consciousness' approach to learning more about a particular piece of work. My friend the late Douglas Hill would let ideas pour out of him after the initial inspiration for a story had struck. Any piece of information that seemed connected with that first idea would be recorded so that eventually 'the world of the story' emerged from the larger mass of material. This of course is not 'how to do it', but it is how Doug did it – and very effectively too, with over 80 books to his credit. He told me once that in order to write a 30,000-word children's novel he might easily generate over 100,000 words' worth of ideas. That's a lot of work; although Doug in common with many writers firmly believed that ultimately no ideas are wasted and that something discarded during the polishing of one story might well find its way into another.

Working methods

My own working method is to think through a project carefully, making notes until a general plan of action becomes clear. Eventually I feel that I can launch into the writing – and it is at least as much of a feeling as it is a conscious understanding that I know enough to tackle the work. At times I'm wrong about this: the book strands itself on the rocks and I have to go back and think again. But that's what experience is all about, though I'm glad to say it happens less frequently now. Again this is not how to do it but it is how I do it; it's a method that works for me. One element of getting children to think like writers is to encourage them to think more independently as they devise (or modify) strategies to suit their own needs and requirements.

You might well object that this noble aim sounds rather time-consuming within a content-laden, results-driven curriculum. Where can we create the opportunities for children to develop their own best practice for writing? It's a fair point. However I argue that it can be achieved within the context of the day-to-day delivery of facts and ideas in different subject areas.

Having suggested that there are any number of 'working methods' for writing and that individual writers tend to create their own over time, after many years in the classroom I have found there are core principles establishing a common ground that contributes to an ethos valuing the power of words and the beauty of language.

Language is power

The effective use of language makes one more powerful. The educationalist Kieran Egan uses the hero-villain polarity to help both classroom practitioners and children appreciate the importance and value of accurate writing (in *Teaching As Story Telling* – see Bibliography). The 'heroic element' of the writing process is clarity of communication. A clear, accurate communication is more influential, impressive and interesting than one which is vague, tortuous and confused. The villain of the piece is represented by the idea that a poor appreciation of language impoverishes the imagination, oversimplifies the world and increases the tendency for the individual to be manipulated by the words of others. It has been well said that people think only in directions for which they have words. If you can increase children's capability to use language for themselves and reflect on the words of others then you supply them not only with a richer life-map but also with a whole raft of orienteering skills.

Language is beautiful

Language is a beautiful and wonderful thing. Not only does learning to develop as a writer refine the sensibilities and intensify one's enjoyment of language per se, it also opens up doorways into many avenues of understanding that would otherwise remain closed or obscure.

Language is freedom

The practical value of boosting linguistic intelligence (above and beyond just being literate in a utilitarian sense) is a truism. Even in an increasingly visual world the capacity to 'process' words is vital. Consider how difficult life would be if one's grasp of language – and therefore of the underlying concepts it conveys – was poor. Such a consideration is no mere academic exercise. An article posted on the Guardian website in May 2010* asserts that one in five adults in the UK is functionally illiterate (although perhaps that should be non-functionally illiterate?). Apart from being disadvantaged in all kinds of ways when this is the case, not least in competing for jobs, a search on the internet pulls up many indications of the correlation between illiteracy and crime. If we go even some way towards accepting the evidence for this, the difference between being able to use language poorly or well has profound consequences for the direction one's life can take.

* www.guardian.co.uk/commentisfree/2010/may/03/illiteracy-innumeracy-prisons

Language is enjoyable

Playing with words is fun. This point (to employ a cliché – but it does a good job) comes last but not least. Perhaps it should have come first. Only in the most tragic circumstances is any child denied the opportunity to explore words, savour them, play with them, learn more about them. The richness of the language environment influences a child's capacity to use language richly. I suggest that cultivating a love of words and encouraging children to use them creatively is their right and our duty.

Practically speaking, and despite the enthusiasm we might bring to the challenge, perhaps not all children will learn to 'think like writers' to the extent that we would wish. But if a child who currently 'doesn't do writing' actually comes to enjoy putting pen to paper even sometimes, then we can be pleased with that success. Beyond this, we can take even greater pride in our achievement if a young writer is inspired as much as Douglas Hill obviously was. During one of his school visits a ten-year-old boy asked him, 'Mr Hill, why do you write?' To which Doug replied, 'Son, why do you breathe?' The more children develop the skill set needed to be writers, the more they realise their inheritance.

Using this book

The intention of this book is to offer classroom practitioners a bagful of practical activities to help children think about writing, coupled with insights into the attitude which I feel is essential if they are to develop their abilities with the aim of fulfilling their potential as writers.

The broad structure of the book follows the pattern of 'thinking time – writing time – looking back/ checking time' and so the activities and techniques can be used sequentially. Alternatively you might prefer just to dip in and try out individual activities to suit the particular aspect of writing you are working on with your class, the time you have available and so on. Dipping in to try out ideas is also fine, with the proviso that different techniques and approaches may suit some young writers better than others. Therefore feel free to adapt, extend, invent or discard freely – this being an important aspect of the creative attitude encouraged throughout.

You will see that some of the activities are addressed to you the teacher, while others are written as though directed at the children themselves. I use this style where I think the particular way you frame the instructions to the class will have a direct bearing on the ease with which children can try the technique and the success of the outcomes.

The activities are aimed at Key stage 2 children but will work equally well at lower Key Stage 3. Some of the techniques are suitable for KS1. I've indicated where I think this is the case, but KS1 specialists will no doubt find creative ways of adapting more!.

2
Inspiration, imagination and motivation

What is inspiration?

'My deepest fears, secrets and emotions inspire me to write.'

Hollie, age 15

Key concept

Children are often keen to know what inspires authors. This frequently translates as 'where do you get your ideas?'. The focus of this chapter is to explore the notion of inspiration more deeply and to help young writers to realise that inspiration is not 'a gift from the gods' (as was believed in classical times) but the active engagement of the writer with the world of the story (poem, play etc).

Learning benefits

- **A growing understanding that the 'locus of control' for inspiration lies largely within the individual.**
- **An awareness that inspiration is an attitude that incorporates curiosity, active interest, excitement and the intention to create something new.**
- **The realisation that self-belief and the urge to write allow one to be inspired more frequently and bring the act of inspiration increasingly under conscious control. (So although inspiration in the form of new ideas can simply 'strike' from the outside, the expectation that it will happen also has a powerful positive effect in making it so.)**

Activities

1. Defining inspiration

Ask children to write down what they mean by the word inspire/inspiration and see if there is any general agreement as to a definition from these ideas. Select key words or phrases that contribute to a deeper understanding of what is actually a complex and multi-faceted experience. At the start of this chapter, Hollie tells us that strong emotions inspire her to write. Examples offered by other young writers include: suddenly having a new thought; admiring someone (who has either succeeded, or who battles on in the face of difficulty); motivation; excitement; knowing you can do it, knowing what to do, enjoying what you do, enthusiasm, ideas coming to you 'out of the blue'; being interested in everything and noticing what you think.

2. **Exploring inspiration**

   Ask children for their views on statements, such as those below, that explore what inspiration might be (my own opinions are bracketed).

   - Inspiration is something you can't control (Inspiration comes more under your control as your creative attitude develops – see chapters 2 and 5 – and you gain in experience).

   - Just as some people are naturally very clever, so some people are naturally always inspired (There's strong evidence to suggest that intelligence is plastic not fixed – see Carol Dweck's *Self-Theories*, for example. Similarly, the degree to which anyone can be inspired can be largely determined by the individual. By the end of this book children should know how to do this!).

   - You have to be clever to be inspired. (See above. Also, what more useful words can children think of in talking about being inspired? The activity above should provide some suggestions).

   - You can be inspired more often if you work hard at your writing (I say 'yes' to this. Effort coupled with the will to learn from experience, including setbacks, brings a deeper sense of achievement. Such an attitude combined with a toolbox of strategies for generating ideas feeds inspiration).

3. **Communicating enthusiasm**

   Invite children to make a brief presentation to the class about a book, film, hobby etc that they really like. The aim of the activity is not to try and persuade anyone to enjoy the same thing, but for a child to communicate why he or she is so enthusiastic or inspired. Presentations of a couple of minutes work well. Encourage children to plan what they will say and not make it up as they go along. Mini-presentations can be used as lesson openers or as a way of rounding off a session.

'Just about anything inspires me to write. The first thing is the sound of words, the rhythms you can make by stringing them together. When I was a kid I loved Martin Luther King's 'I have a dream' speech and the little poems Muhammad Ali wrote. Then there was music. I grew up with the Beatles, Dusty Springfield, Bob Dylan, Sam Cooke, reggae and soul. A lot of great songs tell great stories. Finally there are the books I read, the films I saw and the odd great event I see on the television news. Basically, it is stories in all their shapes, forms and varieties.'

Alan Gibbons, author.

Stories are everywhere

'If history were taught in the form of stories, it would never be forgotten.'

Rudyard Kipling (1865–1936) English writer and poet

Key concept

Kipling's assertion touches on the important notion that as human beings we cannot help but create stories. One reason for this is that they give structure to our lives, but at least as importantly, they highlight the human drama that is often the core characteristic of our experiences, both actually and vicariously through the stories we read and watch.

Although we all understand this more or less implicitly, writers exploit the universal nature and structure of story – the use of heroes and villains, problems, journeys and resolutions. They concentrate human drama so that the senses are enriched and the emotions excited, but however fantastical the narrative it must connect with the lives of their readers.

> Learning benefits
> - **Encourages the notion that because the 'raw material' for stories is all around us, being stuck for something to write about is a state of mind rather than a lack of imagination.**
> - **Personalises the learning by linking the craft of story making to the children's own everyday thoughts, observations and experiences.**

Activities

Ask the children to –

1. **Collecting snippets**
   Notice snippets of conversation, meetings between people etc that you come across in your day-to-day lives. What might have led them up to that point? What might happen next? Either swap ideas with your friends or jot down a few notes.

2. **How believable**
   Using one or two of your ideas above, draw a line on a piece of paper and make a 1–5 scale: 1 means the story is ordinary and everyday, 5 means it's incredible, amazing, fantastic. Where would you put your idea(s) along that line? Take one idea and 'push it further along the line'. What changes? If you carried on that story, where could it lead?

3. **Spin a yarn**
   Get into the habit of weaving little stories out of the simplest things. Look around you. Suppose you saw a pencil, a cup and a newspaper. If these three things appeared in an exciting story, what would that story be? Explain it in just a sentence if you can.

4. The linking game

Use the linking technique above to create lots of story ideas quickly. Look at the items on the previous page. Pick two or three:

- If you used them in a story, what would that story be about? Explain in one sentence if possible.
- Now, using the same objects, change the genre and think of a new story idea.
- Ask a friend to pick one more object to add to your selection. How does this new object change or add to the story?

Take it further

1. Stones as lessons

Do you agree with what Rudyard Kipling said? Explain why. What do you think he meant by 'the form of stories'? Do you think other factual subjects could be taught that way?

2. Gee whiz facts

Make a short list of 'gee whiz' facts about science, history, English – or your hobbies and pastimes. In other words, facts and ideas that have amazed you. Why are these ideas interesting do you think?

3. Lesson planner

Working with a group of friends, plan out what would be an exciting, unforgettable lesson for your class using a topic of your choice.

'Everybody walks past a thousand story ideas every day. The good writers are the ones who see five or six of them. Most people don't see any.'

Orson Scott Card, American author

Being nosy – noticing

''Ever since I have grown an interest in writing, my ways of looking at things have changed. When I do the simplest thing like walking down a road I think about every single detail which is going into it, so that I could make the most boring thing interesting to read.'

Bita Yazdani, 16

Key concept

Observation is a key skill, not just to finding ideas for writing, but also for collecting the vivid details that can immediately make writing more memorable. Use of vivid details helps writers to 'show' rather than just 'tell' – in other words, to put the reader through an experience that the writer himself has had, or in fiction that a character is having.

Learning benefits

- **Develops a key skill that can be used in many other learning contexts.**
- **Boosts confidence in so far as all children are able to notice things. Related activities can be pitched at any level of challenge depending upon the age and ability of the group.**

Activities

1. Be nosy

Ask the children to notice something about familiar surroundings that they haven't noticed before – at home, in school, in their neighbourhood etc. Examples from a Year 5/6 class include –

- I noticed a pinky-orange rose in my garden even though it was 1 November.
- I noticed that the skin around my Grandma's eyes crinkles when she smiles.
- I noticed that the iron gate to the path at the front of the house does a double squeak when you open it.
- I noticed a sweet smell in the toiletries aisle at the local supermarket.
- I noticed that Ben who sits next to me in class has light blue-grey eyes.

(Suitable for KS1)

2. Mini descriptions

Look at the characters below. Pick a few and write a one-sentence description for each of them.

Case study

Here are some attempts by a Year 6 group:

Top left – long oval faced man, receding hair, strong nose and scary eyes.

Top middle – lady with long wavy fairish hair and a scornful expression.

Top right – smart, bird-faced man with slicked-back straight dark hair.

Bottom left – pale smooth-skinned lady, curly fringe and unhappy eyes.

Bottom middle – round-faced balding man, thin dark moustache and sneering expression.

Bottom right – young woman with straight dark hair, pointed chin and alert wide eyes.

3. Thumbnail characters

Now do the same with real people you see around you. Look for a few details of each person's face, voice, the way they walk etc and write some 'thumbnail' character descriptions. (Remember to be respectful at all times!)

4. Characters in stories

Use the information you have gathered to create some fictional characters to use in stories or just as a way of improving your descriptive writing. Here are some ideas you can try –

- Coin flip characters. Ask yes-no questions about a character and flip a coin to get the answers. You can ask about the character's physical appearance, family and friends, personality and lifestyle. You'll invent some interesting people this way – but remember characters need to be convincing so you may decide to change some of the answers.

- Personality profile. Take a sheet of A4 paper and draw ten lines across on the right hand side, spaced equally down the page. At the top of the page on the right draw a line numbered from 1 to 6. Now on the left of the page, beside each line put an adjective that describes a characteristic feature of the personality. So you might choose friendly, intelligent, kind, mischievous, brave etc. Roll a dice for each characteristic. If for example you roll 3 for friendly, make a mark halfway along the line opposite that word. Roll for each characteristic to create an interesting personality profile. Some parts of the character's personality may not seem to agree or fit. For example, you may find that a character is very unkind but really popular. You can either challenge yourself by thinking of an explanation, or simply decide to alter one of the scores (the easy way out!).

- Naming characters. The first bit of advice is not to try hard to think of names as they might sound forced and artificial. Secondly, do not to use the names of your friends or people you know. Apart from the fact that they might not approve of what you say, when you write about your characters you'll probably always have your friends in mind who may be nothing like the characters in the story. Here are some ideas for finding natural-sounding names:

- Use the library to find six ordinary-sounding first names from any of the books. Number the names from 1 to 6. Now do the same for surnames. Use dice rolls to match a first name with a surname. Notice the result.

- Discuss whether/how some people are suited to their names. For instance I know someone called Jack who has a cheeky sense of humour (maybe I'm linking this with the idea of 'Jack the lad'?).

- To make up names for fantasy and science fiction stories, take a line of text and begin matching up the last syllable of one word with the first syllable of the next. So in the last sentence we get – Toma, Akeu, Upna, Esfo, Orfa, Asyan, Riesta, Keal, etc. Some will sound better than others of course.

- Look at names in literature – Dickens is a great source. What characters do you imagine from their names? Where did authors get their characters' names? Check out James Bond, Sherlock Holmes, Tracey Beaker.

5. Noticing yourself

Experienced writers often give the advice 'show don't tell'. So for example if in a story you write that your character is frightened, you have simply told your reader that is the case. 'Showing' the reader means trying to give him or her the experience of fear that the character is feeling. One way of doing this is to notice yourself as you experience different feelings – or at least afterwards by remembering them. Notice the posture of your body. What about the speed and depth of your breathing? Your pulse rate? What muscles are tense? Think about your facial expression. With this information you can write much more vividly, so that your readers 'live through' the experiences your characters have but more powerfully.

Teacher tip

Using one's own (even unpleasant) experiences creatively in writing is an example of the general principle that nothing is ever wasted.

Take it further

1. Coming to your senses

Practise noticing with your other senses. As you walk down the street, notice sounds, smells and the textures of things. How would you put them into words? Develop your skill by feeling two things that are made of similar materials. How would you explain the difference to someone? Or listen to two cats purring – describe the sounds. Make a list of challenges that you and your friends can try out. Here are some to start you off:

- The difference in taste between two varieties of apple.
- The difference between being annoyed and being quite cross.
- The difference in engine sound between a bus and a truck.
- The difference in shade between the blonde hair of two fair-haired people.
- The difference in texture between two kinds of paper.

2. **One of a kind**

Noticing differences helps us to appreciate the individuality or uniqueness of people, places and things. This is not just a matter of appearance, but that's a good place to start.

Look at a tree, for instance. Can you spot one thing that makes it different somehow from trees of a similar kind? Looking at the natural world offers many more examples. Notice the sky. In five minutes it will have changed. Can you describe the particular colour of the light on or within the clouds, the way the clouds are moving, the general appearance of the sky as it is right now?

The Victorian Jesuit poet Gerard Manley Hopkins defined the uniqueness of something by the word 'inscape', while its expression in the world he referred to as 'instress'. W. H. Gardner's Introduction to a selection of Hopkins' poetry and prose lucidly explores how the poet tried to describe the individuality of things in his work (see Bibliography).

'Take the first difficult step of actually writing something rather than just thinking about it. Write and write and don't worry about whether it's good or not until you've finished your first draft.'

Barbara Gidman, author

Being nosy – questioning

'The important thing is not to stop questioning. Curiosity has its own reason for existing.'

Albert Einstein (1879–1955) German theoretical physicist

Key concept

No one can doubt the value of asking questions as part of the learning process. They demonstrate the active wish to find out more. In the classroom 'low level' questioning is often closed however and such questions when asked by the teacher are usually to check that knowledge has been remembered. Closed questions asked by children are frequently 'procedural': 'Shall I write this in my best book?', 'Is the homework in for Wednesday?' etc. High level questioning however is usually more open, incisive and increasingly initiated by the children in an active search for clearer meanings and

---

greater understanding. This is the kind of questioning that characterises a creative attitude and is an expression of the sophisticated thinking that underpins effective writing.

Learning benefits

- **Shifts the emphasis of thinking more towards the learner.**
- **Implicitly values the thinking of every child who asks a question.**
- **Engages interest in so far as children will come to ask questions of greater relevance to themselves and the task in hand.**
- **Provides useful feedback for the teacher as to the degree of understanding that children have already reached.**

Activities

1. Questions for characters

Look back at the characters on page 9. Pick a character and create a list of questions that would help you to learn more about that person. Remember the 'Five Ws and the H': who, what, where, when, why, how. You can also make up questions that can be answered yes or no, such as 'Is this person married?', 'Is this person going on a journey?'

2. Sorting questions

Rank your list of questions according to how much each one helps you to learn about your character. For instance, the answer to the question 'Why does this person look so angry?' would tell you more than 'Does this person have brown eyes?' Discard any questions that you think aren't really relevant (but see also activity 6).

Teacher tip

Diamond ranking. Explain to the groups that their list for relevance does not have to be entirely linear. Invite the children to write each question on a piece of paper or card and physically arrange them on the table. If two questions are judged to be of equal relevance they will be placed side by side. This technique is known as diamond ranking, see next page.

---

3. Creating believable answers

Swap your list of questions with another group. Discuss your new list and create answers to the questions. Follow these rules –

- Answers must not be silly or inappropriate.
- The answers must not contradict each other. For example the two answers 'This person is having a really bad day' and 'This person is very happy' don't seem to fit. However, if you can think of a strong reason why they do fit then you will not have broken the rule.

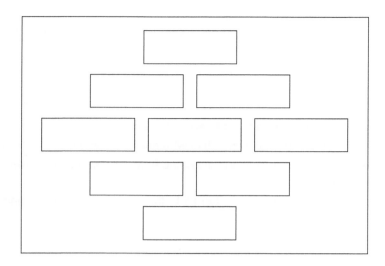

4. Responses and reasons

Now swap your lists of questions back. Look at the answers to the yes/no (closed) questions you asked – or if you didn't ask any think of some now. You can answer them yourself, making sure they fit the answers to the other questions. If the other group have answered any questions with just a yes or a no, think of a reason to fit the answer. So if you asked 'Does this person wear scruffy clothes?' and the answer was yes, make up a reason why this is the case. Make sure the reason fits with what else you have learned about your character.

Take it further

5. A handful of reasons

Test your imagination further by thinking of several explanations for the yes-no answers you looked at in activity 4. So if you learned that your character wears scruffy clothes you might suggest:–

- because (s)he has no job or money
- because (s)he is doing some decorating at home
- because (s)he is going to a fancy dress party
- because (s)he is a spy undercover
- because (s)he has just escaped from a collapsing building.

Notice how each of these explanations is like a doorway that opens up further possible story ideas. You can easily develop the story by asking more questions.

6. Exploring relevance

Look back at activity 2 and find those questions that you thought weren't relevant or at all important. For each question, think of a situation where the answer *would be* really significant in a story or situation. For example, suppose you discarded the question 'Does this person have brown eyes?' Let's pretend the answer is 'yes'. Think of a situation (or more than one!) where that character having brown eyes is important in a story. Having done that, pretend the answer is 'no'. Think of a couple more situations where the character not having brown eyes is important.

7. How language influences

This quick task shows you another example of how authors choose what they say and how they say it for reasons they've thought about. Read the newspaper headline and jot down anything you notice about how it's been written. Discuss possible reasons why the writer has done things this way.

Now the government makes it **even HARDER** to sell your home!!

Suggestions:

- 'Now' suggests that the government has done other things to make life difficult for people.
- '**even**' suggests it has been hard to sell your home in the past, but that things are now worse. The word written in bold makes it stand out more.
- '**HARDER**' written in capitals and bold reinforces the points above and the attitude of the newspaper towards the government. The fact that the letters are capitals also suggest loudness driven by strong feelings – that's why it is considered bad manners to email or text in capitals, because it looks like you are SHOUTING. Writing it this way also hooks your attention and makes the word/the whole headline stick in your memory for longer.
- 'your' makes it personal – this is being done to you.
- 'home' is a warmer, cosier word than 'house' and also more personal. Contrast 'your home' with the phrase 'a property'.

- The double exclamation marks suggest anger or outrage. Notice that although the rules of punctuation say you should use exclamation marks sparingly, and that it is incorrect to use more than one together, the headline writer has decided to bend the rules for a reason he or she has thought about.

Teacher tip

The Japanese haiku poet Basho supposedly said in the context of his work, 'Learn the rules well and then you can bend them'. There is an opportunity here to discuss bending or breaking grammatical rules for a considered purpose.

---

8. Categorising questions

Many children understand the distinction between closed and open questions. In this section we have also grouped according to relevance. Ask the class if they can come up with other categories, or add some detail to categories or sample questions they have already come across. For instance –

- Big idea questions and little idea questions (What new inventions might exist in 100 years time?, What colour shirt will I choose to wear today?).
- Questions that have one right or agreed answer, those that could be said to have many right answers, questions that have not been answered yet, questions that may be unanswerable.

Teacher tip

Looking at questions in this way helps prepare the way for running philosophical enquiries with the class. Philosophy for Children (P4C) is actively growing across the UK and abroad. For more information and some excellent resources go to www.sapere.org.uk

---

- Questions sorted according to function. For example: recalling information; eliciting further information; challenging opinions or assumptions; making connections; deciding actions. For more information see Morgan & Saxton, *Asking Better Questions* in the Bibliography.
- Questions matrix. This was designed by Chuck Weiderhold in 1991 and is a useful tool in helping children to generate further questions of their own. 'Put 'Question Matrix' into a search engine to see Weiderhold's template.' (or similar).

Teacher tip

Using questions to help children improve their writing at the editing stage is explored on page 104 in Bita's story.

3
Critical thinking

Be a detective – a reasoning game

Key concept

Noticing and questioning are precursors to various forms of reasoning. Within the context of earlier ideas the activities below reinforce the idea for young writers that everything happening in a story is there for a reason that has been considered. This basic principle can operate at any level from, say, the basic structure of the plot or character motivations, to why a certain street name has been used.

Everything there for a reason

- The 'everything there for a reason' guideline should not in my view take precedence over encouraging children simply to enjoy their writing. When children have to try and remember too many rules the creative flow will be inhibited and 'overwhelm' can take over; a kind of locking up of the writing process because there's just too much to think about and get right. At the stage of simply pouring out one's thoughts on to the page or screen, even insisting on correct spelling, punctuation and neatness might be too distracting or off-putting – although these matters are important ultimately. An understanding of rules and correct procedure can be applied at the redrafting/editing stage and in any case will grow out of experience. A more experienced young author will apply a whole raft of rules to a high standard of exactness as he or she writes for pleasure. In other words, get the motivation and confidence going and eventually children will want to use the rules effectively anyway to make their work the best that it can be.

- Apply the principle of things happening for reasons at the redrafting/editing stage as a way of improving the writing. As children look back over their work you can prompt them to wonder why a certain character's name was chosen or a particular choice of words was selected for a conversation. Initially a child might say 'I don't know' or 'There's no reason'. Try replying with 'Pretend you do know and tell me when you're ready.' Or 'If there was a reason, what would it be?' – and see what happens. Bear in mind though that trying to pin a reason on everything can be tedious: use a light touch in helping children to become familiar with the idea.

- Raise awareness of the power of the principle of reasons by applying it in other subject areas. It is a useful analytical tool when studying other texts (why did the author use that image?), and in science, art, geography etc.
- Emphasise the 'thinking skills' that underpin the basic act of looking for reasons. Most obviously these are –
  - Speculating – generating possible explanations based on the clues or evidence given (with an understanding that there is a big 'maybe' factor involved).
  - Assuming – reacting to clues or evidence that are not in fact present, or 'jumping to a conclusion' in the absence of supporting evidence.
  - Inferring – reaching a conclusion based on evidence. Often inferences become stronger (or are discarded) as more supporting evidence is gathered.

Learning benefits
- **Reinforces the importance of noticing and questioning.**
- **Introduces and develops a range of key thinking skills.**
- **Offers techniques that give children greater control over the use of their imagination.**

Activities

Again, enhance children's effectiveness in thinking in these ways by applying them in other subject / topic areas. Introduce or revisit them now in the 'Be a detective game' below.

1. Be a detective

The basic game is to present the class with a list of clues and ask what might have happened.

  a. The back door leading to the kitchen is open.
  b. A teacloth is lying on the kitchen floor.
  c. A plate on the worktop has no food on it.
  d. There are grease marks on the plate and on the worktop around it.
  e. The family dog does not appear when called.

Teacher tip

From the outset ask children to sequence their thoughts, explaining what they think might have happened as though watching a movie.

Using the pieces of evidence above, a common scenario is that the family dog either came in through the open back door, or was inside the house anyway. He smelt the food on the plate, wrestled the teacloth covering the food on to the floor and ate the food, leaving greasy prints in the process. Then he went out and hid guiltily when one of the family called to him.

There are several ways of developing this game.

2. Gathering clues

Ask each child or group to write another short clue on a scrap of paper. Put the scraps in a bag, pull them out one at a time and discuss how the new evidence influences people's ideas about what happened. Note: the new clues need not be based on any previous scenario. One way of ensuring this, is to give the children/groups 'prompt words' that influence their thinking. These too can be written on scraps of paper or card. Examples are: murder, kidnap, sleepover, Hallowe'en, birthday, salesman, removal van etc. So for instance one class when given the prompt 'kidnap' came up with these extra clues –

- A note in a stranger's handwriting is pinned to the corkboard in the kitchen.
- There are four missed calls on the answer machine in the hall.
- The family dog has a rare pedigree.
- The older brother has fallen in with a criminal gang.
- A small table in the lounge is on its side.
- The lock on the back door has been forced.

3. Alternative scenarios

If the class as a whole is given a prompt word like 'childnap' they will produce new clues like those above. Once you have a good collection, ask the children to come up with other scenarios using most or all of the clues – but stress that the scenarios must have nothing to do with kidnapping. This is a creative challenge in so far as it stretches children's thinking and asks them to go beyond the obvious or likely.

4. Three-step questioning

Highlight assumptions in the original set of clues and or the new ones. Ask the children to consider the so-called 'three step' process of questioning:

- What do we actually know?
- What do we think we know?
- What questions can we ask to find out more?

The first question encourages a re-examination of the evidence and 'primes' the reader to look for assumptions and inferences. The second question asks for these to be made explicit, out of which understanding come further questions that take the enquiry forward. In the scenario we have been using it is commonly assumed that –

- There was originally food on the plate.
- The grease marks came from the food.
- The dog was responsible for eating the food.
- The dog left the grease marks on the worktop.

On reflection we see that we only thought we knew that these were so, when in fact none of them might be true. Questions for the third stage of the three-step process might be open or closed. This is a good opportunity to revisit the big question words of where, when, what, why, who and how.

If children ask closed questions (such as 'Did the dog have anything to do with what happened?') flip a coin to get a yes or no answer. Use this as a way of formulating further questions. So if 'yes' a pertinent question would be 'Did the dog eat food that was on the plate?' If 'no' a relevant question would be 'Was there any food on the plate to begin with?'

5. How likely?

Ask the children to imagine a scale of 1–5. The scenario of the dog eating the food would be 1 on the scale. Now ask for scenarios that would be 2 on the scale, then 3 etc – 5 might involve aliens, wizards or (the favourite of many boys) zombies. The value of this technique is that it provides a way of 'reining in' the imagination. Many children seem automatically to leap towards the wacky or fantastical in their writing. Sometimes this is appropriate and sometimes not. A farfetched incident in a narrative is not necessarily any more original than one that is mundane or prosaic. The 'how likely' tool stops children's imaginations from 'running away with them' and offers thinking time that reduces the tendency for children to grab at the first idea that comes to mind.

6. Genre overlay

Another variation of the detective game is to place the thinking within a genre. Using the original set of clues, tell the class that they are part of a romance story. What new scenarios can they now invent? Then suggest the clues are part of a fantasy story, then a spy thriller etc. Develop the idea by using words and pictures related to a particular genre drawn on to scraps of paper. Place these in an envelope and draw them out one at a time. Let the class create new scenarios that incorporate these motifs as they appear.

The magic of imagination

'Imagination rules the world.'

Napoleon Bonaparte (1769–1821) French military and political leader

---

Key concept

Imagination has been defined as the ability to create mental scenarios that need have nothing to do with our immediate circumstances. We all possess this astonishing ability, but just as we develop strength, stamina and power in our bodies, so too does the imagination benefit from systematic exercise and increasing challenge.

(I am still shocked and disappointed to encounter adults who tell me that particular children or even whole classes 'have no imagination'. This is not only patently absurd but can be massively damaging. Even if the person concerned doesn't say it aloud, he will behave as if it were true, with the same detrimental consequences.)

Learning benefits

- **Develops metacognitive ability (the capacity we have to notice and influence our own thoughts).**
- **Increases the vividness and detail of children's thinking, which often immediately lifts the quality of their writing in terms of its richness.**
- **Boosts confidence in so far as children come to realise more clearly that through imagination they can learn to generate, organise and refine their ideas with increasing effectiveness. This in itself can be highly motivational in prompting children to put pen to paper.**

Activities

1. Just imagine

Here are a few simple activities that help children to internalise their awareness, develop concentration and increase conscious control of the imagination.

- Close your eyes and imagine the classroom where you are sitting. After 30 seconds open your eyes and compare your mental image with the room itself. Notice something you imagined exactly. Notice something that you imagined differently in some way. Notice something in the room that you failed to imagine.

Teacher tip

For this next activity allow thinking time of around ten seconds between each instruction. As you ask children to imagine more complex objects or sequences of movement increase the time you give them to do it. This helps to develop concentration in preparation for the 'metacognitive dialogue' activity on page 26.

- Close your eyes again. Imagine a place where you like to be (which can include your classroom if you want!). Just let yourself settle in the place so that you feel comfortable there. Now imagine a white tennis ball on the ground in front of you. Reach out and pick it up. Feel the texture of its surface. Squeeze the ball and notice how it has just a little bit of give. Change the colour of the ball. Change it again. Make it multicoloured. Bounce the ball on the ground, catching it each time at the top of the bounce. Notice the sound it makes as it hits the floor. Spin it on the end of your finger. Keep it spinning. Now withdraw your finger and keep the ball spinning by itself in mid air. As it spins, enlarge it to the size of a football. Make it bigger still. Now shrink it down and down to the size of a grape. Then smaller still until you can barely see it. Turn it back into an ordinary-sized tennis ball. Make it white again. Stop it spinning. Make it vanish in a puff of purple smoke.

Creating and manipulating visual images will be easier for some children than for others. By the same token, other children will find imagining sounds or textures easier. This tendency to favour one sensory mode is often reflected in a child's writing. A more visually-orientated thinker may well put plenty of visual description in his work, but auditory and tactile references might be sparse. Practising this kind of multisensory visualisation develops the habit of giving all sensory modes equal weight (to use a tactile reference!). As a result the children's writing should become richer with this greater variety of details.

2. Writing visualisations

You can apply the 1–5 scale used on page 20. The tennis ball visualisation above begins at 1 but shifts towards a fantastical 5. Most children will have fun imagining fantastic or impossible things, but intersperse these visualisations with ones that are of ordinary everyday things.

3. In the right order

Extend the visualisation to help improve instructional writing.

Ask each child or group to write brief and clear instructions for carrying out a simple procedure such as making a cup of tea. From time to time, use the children's examples and run a visualisation activity (remembering to build in thinking time between each instruction). Sequence the sets of instructions from simpler to more complex. As this imagination-training programme progresses, encourage the children to visualise an entire process before writing anything down. Once they've finished, ask them to re-read the instructions, checking their accuracy against the earlier visualisation.

4. Imagination and the senses

Enhance descriptive writing through the power of visualisation.

Use a simple black and white sketch like the illustration below. Ask the children to 'step into' the image so that (in this case) they are standing in the desert watching the man on the horse from afar.

- Now 'turn up' the colours of the landscape. Use your judgement as to how far you direct what the children are to visualise. You might say 'Notice the colours of the landscape' or be more prescriptive with 'Notice the reddish-yellow sand and the deeper orangey-red of the mesa.'

Teacher tip

If you decide not to be very prescriptive, obviously children will differ as to the details they imagine. It is important to emphasise to the class that no one is right or wrong in how their imagination works: Taylor's greyish-white desert is just as valid as Lucy's golden yellow one. However, if a child tells you that the sand is bright pink use the 'everything for a reason' principle (see page 14). My response would be to say 'Your mind has given you that idea. If you decide to use it in your work, then the sand will have to be pink for a reason that you've thought about and which makes the work better. When you've thought of a good reason, tell it to me. Or you might choose to change the colour of the sand.' Perhaps the child is just being silly or deliberately trying to irritate, or possibly she has not yet developed sufficient control over her imagination. Framing your reply in this way however is non-judgemental, values the thinking that the child has done and allows her to 'step away with dignity'. Of course, she might decide to keep the pink sand and offer a reason that you find convincing.

- Now 'turn up' the sounds as you stand there in the desert. Again you can judge how much to feed the children with ideas such as the slow, distant clop-clop of the horse's hooves, perhaps insects (cicadas?) nearby, maybe the clatter of loose stones tumbling down the nearby cliffs.

- Feel the heat of the sun. I Imagine where it is in the sky. The desert has a dusty smell. Pick up a handful of the dusty sand and a few small stones. Feel their texture.
- Now begin walking towards the distant rider (noticing the soft sound of your shoes on the ground). The horse stops as you approach. Notice further colours, sounds. The rider speaks. Notice the qualities of his own – speed, pitch, volume, tone.
- A useful trick of the imagination is to become the character you're visualising. Imagine you are the rider sitting on the horse. Where have you been? Where are you going? How do you feel? This kind of visualisation is a precursor to the more extended and sophisticated metacognitive dialogue described on page 25.

Teacher tip

Occasionally a child may not want to become an imagined character or take part in a visualisation. I rarely ask why and always let the child get on with some other activity or errand.

Take it further

1. Think film

Use the vocabulary of film making to increase the challenge. Working with words or a picture, ask the class to manipulate images in their mind in the following ways –

BCU	Big close up	**Mix**	Blending one picture into another
Cut	Changing from one scene to another	**Pan**	Moving panoramicallay up / down or sideways
Fade	Turning up or down sound / picture	**POV**	Point of view
Long Shot	View showing the whole scene	**Zoom**	Drawing away or closer-in

Practising metacognitive dialogue

In the case of one young writer, Lauren, having 'stepped into' the desert scene above we asked her to imagine slow-panning 360°. This is an extract from the conversation she had with her teacher.

L: I'm turning slowly around to the right. The cliffs get higher and I can see buzzards flying above them… No not flying, kind of gliding. The cliffs curve away to my left. Now I can see a few cactuses.

T: Are there any nearby?

L: Yes, a tall one with – do you call them branches? – sticking out a bit like arms.

T: Go over to it and tell me more.

L: OK I'm walking towards it. It's at least twice as tall as I am. It's lightish green but there are patches of yellow and brown, maybe where the skin has been damaged. It has like clusters of long spines (breaks her own concentration at this point and looks at her teacher) I'm thinking of a cactus we've got at home. It's only little and it's round, but has the same kind of spines.

T: That's fine. Are the spines on the desert cactus longer?

L: (Eyes move away as she concentrates again) Yes, a bit longer than my middle finger but much thinner. And the spines are grey.

T: Touch the skin of the cactus. What do you notice?

L: (Reaches out her hand to touch the imaginary cactus) Um, I can push it in a bit – like when you press an orange. I've pushed near where the skin is broken. A bit of juice oozes out. It glistens in the sun…

Lauren was able to hold the desert scene in her mind for over ten minutes and, with the teacher's gentle prompting, drew out some vivid details from which she could subsequently select when writing her description of 'The rider in the desert'. I have called this technique 'metacognitive dialogue' and we'll look at it further in the next chapter.

2. Time-lapse thinking

An interesting refinement of the technique above is to play with time. Most children will have seen time-lapse movies, for example of flowers growing, while slow motion is a common (perhaps overused) feature of many modern action films. Once your young writers have had some experience of visualising, try out the following. Imagine…

- A year in the life of an oak tree in the next ten seconds.
- A car abandoned on a piece of waste ground rusting away until it's just a pile of junk.
- A butterfly egg hatching a caterpillar, which at super speed becomes a pupa then a butterfly.
- A rose seedling in the garden sprouting, growing, becoming a rose bush covered in flowers.
- In slow motion, imagine a small pebble dropped into water.
- In slow motion, a bullet passing through an apple.
- In slow motion, a firework exploding in the sky.
- In slow motion, a demolition team blowing up a tall factory chimney.

Teacher tip

YouTube is a great source of such clips. Help children to understand what you want them to imagine by showing them a selection, but leave the visualising until some time later so that they have to actively reconstruct the imagery rather than more easily remembering something they've just seen.

Metacognitive dialogue

'Imagination is the highest kite you can fly.'

Author unknown

Key concept

Metacognition is the ability to notice, reflect on and manipulate one's own thoughts. This skill can be developed quickly through a dialogue which prompts the visualiser to reach beyond the obvious and draw out more details in the imagination.

Learning benefits

- **Improves concentration and the ability to internalise the attention.**
- **Raises awareness of how imagination works at an individual level.**
- **Creates a greater sense of ownership of ideas for a young writer.**
- **Offers a quick and effective technique for generating ideas that form the raw material for subsequent writing.**

In the previous section, we touched on the notion of metacognitive dialogue in the conversation between Lauren and her teacher. We saw how the teacher's role was to gently prompt the visualiser to notice further details in her mind and 'speak them out'. Since children can be taught very quickly to take on this role we might rename it the role of 'prompter'. Below are some guidelines the prompter needs to follow.

The role of the prompter

i. The general attitude is one of interest and gentle encouragement. Typically the dialogue proceeds through asking open questions. These might be about any aspect of the mental scenario that the visualiser has already mentioned. However there is also value in asking for more information over the course of several questions around a single aspect of the scenario. For example, if the visualiser mentions that an imagined character has spoken, the prompter could ask a number of questions about the qualities of the character's voice before moving on to enquire about the content of what was said.

ii. Allow plenty of thinking time. If the visualiser isn't responding it's probably because she is concentrating rather than because she has nothing to say. If the visualiser does say 'I don't know' try replying with 'Well pretend you do and tell me when you've noticed.'

iii. A further bonus of the technique is that the prompter is also using his imagination to picture the scene (and experience its sounds, smells, textures etc). But his scenario will differ from the visualiser's own. Generally speaking, the prompter should not impose his own details on to the visualiser's mental imagery, except obliquely. For instance on page 25 Lauren's teacher asked her if the cactus Lauren was imagining had spines. This question was probably prompted by the fact that the cactus the teacher was imagining had spines. Too much prompting of this kind though can be overly intrusive.

iv. Ask questions that draw out multisensory thinking.

v. If the visualiser doesn't wish to share a thought, then respect that.

vi. Normally a dialogue will run its natural course, but allow the visualiser to end the dialogue at any point.

vii. It's often useful to record dialogues or have a scribe who can make notes.

Activities

1. Metacognitive dialogues

These are usually run between two people. However, a variation of the activity is to use a descriptive sentence or a picture with the whole class, then ask questions but have the children write down their individual responses.

In the street scene below for example, you can say 'Walk down the alley with the store on your right until you come to the car park. Notice how full it is and make a note. A car pulls up and parks. Two people get out. Notice the one who was driving and jot down three details about that person. The passenger says something as they walk past you. Notice three things about that person's voice and make a note. Or listen to what that person says and briefly describe what it was.'

2. Metacognitive association webs

Write a descriptive detail or stick a black and white picture in the middle of a display board and encourage children to notice how they imagine it in terms of colours, sounds, what lies outside the frame etc. This could be an ongoing project where details are added in spare moments over the course of several days, or ask every child to write at least one detail and invite small groups to come up to pin their ideas to the board. One benefit of running the activity through time is that children can add to details previously pinned up.

3. Richer reading

At its simplest this is a greater awareness by the reader of how she/he is imagining what is being read. We all create mental scenarios as we read, most vividly perhaps for fiction and poetry (more abstract text is processed/understood in a less obvious way).

For example, notice how your imagination works as you read the following –

The large Elizabethan house had gone to ruin now. It lay almost forgotten amidst extensive oak woods in a corner of rural England.

As I am more visually oriented in my thinking I see grey stone walls streaked with green from leaky guttering, pale yellow roof tiles and an impression of being closed in by trees and shrubbery. I am close to the wall. I 'know' about the roof tiles but can't see them from where I am standing. There is a sense of sunlight through the leaf canopy, but just here it is chilly and damp.

For me the visual impression came spontaneously, then the more tactile sense of cold and damp. I needed to make an effort of the imagination to hear sounds or smell the undergrowth.

Teacher tip

Notice how this example assumes that the reader knows what an Elizabethan house looks like. It is worth bearing this in mind when working with children. In this case you can either show them pictures of such houses prior to the activity, or prompt them with a few extra details such as 'big old fashioned house', 'lots of windows', 'tall chimneys' etc. Vocabulary might also be an issue. Some children will need to have 'rural' explained to them, as well as the meaning of 'Elizabethan'.

The notion of making an 'effort of the imagination' is an important one. Many of the activities we have already explored encourage thinking time. When children are shown how to notice more details about their imagined characters or settings then they have more 'raw material' to choose from when adding details to their written work. require the writer to allow time for thought, sustain concentration and deliberately add detail to mental scenarios in order to make them richer and more complex. In effect strengthening the imagination is a discipline and I feel a necessary one since thinking precedes writing.

Take it further

The skill of reading with such awareness can be developed through the use of templates such as the one opposite.

Text is placed in the middle column of the page. This might be a child's own work or published material (obtained with permission) that has been copied and pasted in. First impressions are noted in the left-hand column. These will be images, sounds etc that appear spontaneously. The right-hand column can be used more flexibly during or after the first read-through, to ask questions, note points of confusion and generally to record other ideas and pieces of information – which might then enrich the details that can be added on the left side of the page by the effort of imagination mentioned above.

This technique is not intended to be used constantly, but if you revisit the activity on a fairly regular basis then much of the other reading that children do will become a richer experience for them. The template can also be used as an editing/redrafting tool. What details work well? What other sensory references can be included to make the writing more vivid for a greater range of readers? The emphasis is on the quality of the language in so far as it stimulates a reader's imagination. I tell children that effective language is usually simple, straightforward and gets the readers' minds working. This is a criterion of quality that most young writers are able to appreciate.

First impressions:		Questions and other notes:
Elegant Dracula with red silk-linked cape. Slicked back black hair.	The skeleton tripped over Dracula's polished shoe and went sprawling on to the grass. With a shriek of delight the vampire swirled up his cloak, turned and ran away through the trees.	Are there other people nearby? I imagine a park. Characters are going to a party.
Wet grass, glinting. There's a street lamp not far away.	" Hey come back!" Diana yelled after him. " We've got a bone to pick with you!"	Quite a friendly feel to things. Dracula was just up to mischief.
Oak trees, leaves falling. Lots of leaves on the ground.	Eleanor Trent burst into giggles but the skeleton – actually Tommy Hyatt who lived on Acker Street – groaned and winced and held his aching back as he scrambled stiffly to his feet.	Tone is comedy, light hearted fun.
Diana – red hair, strong face.		What costumes are Diana and Eleanor wearing?
Eleanor – younger looking, thinner, blonde hair with red and purple streaks for Halloween.	" I suppose," he said, " you think that's funny?" Eleanor tried to force herself to stop, but the giggles came bubbling up like soda and she had to put a hand over her mouth to hide her mirth. Diana just grinned, and it was such an open friendly grin that Tommy could do nothing but shrug and instantly forgive her.	Friendly feel.
		What sound does the wind make in the trees?
Tommy – a couple of years younger (about 12), short with straight dark hair, skeleton body costume.	" OK, so it was kind of funny…" He dragged off his skull mask. Eleanor thought that his flushed face and tousled hair looked really cute. " Thank you kind ladies for helping a poor old bag-o-bones on this wild and weird night!"	
Windy. Moonlight. Rushing clouds.		What is the smell of the wet leaves and grass?

Note: The extract above is taken from a short story called 'Eleanor's Hand'.

'He who has imagination without learning has wings but no feet.'

Joseph Joubert (1754–1824) French essayist

4
Writing for the love of it

'Fill your paper with the breathings of your heart.'

William Wordsworth (1770–1850) Romantic poet

Interestingly the word 'inspire' is linked to breathing. The Ancient Greeks believed that artists at the moment of inspiration were 'breathed upon' by the Muses. When I talk to children about the word I say that inspiration is about breathing in experiences and breathing out ideas.

Key concept

Not long ago when I was visiting a school a Year 5 boy said to me, after I'd given a talk and shown the group some of my books, 'Oh so you're a professional writer then?' First of all that was a refreshing change from being called a 'real live author' (as though children could not tell the difference). I replied that I tried to be professional in wanting to do my best, setting myself the highest standards I could. But in another equally important sense I was an amateur, given that the root of the word means 'lover of' or 'for the love of'.

Just about every writer I've ever met writes for the love of it. This section aims to emphasise the sheer pleasure of crafting the work and looks at other aspects of how imagination, emotions and the body work together in the act of writing.

Learning benefits

- **Offers a powerful rationale and incentive for engaging with the effort and discipline of writing.**
- **Highlights the fact that writing is not just an intellectual exercise but profoundly involves feelings, beliefs and values.**
- **Suggests the importance of expressing oneself and one's view of the world.**
- **Distinguishes between personal achievement and (usually externally imposed) 'objectified' attainment.**

An important lesson for us as teachers is to encourage and praise the effort, whether or not it leads to 'high' results. Carol Dweck in her book *Self-Theories* explores the deep importance of this and related topics (see Bibliography).

Activities

1. For the love of it

Discuss the attitude of doing something, if not for the love of it, then for enjoyment. Link this with the notion of making an effort to see something through. What if, after all, the project was not a success (having defined the sense in which it was not)? Does that diminish the pleasure and achievement of it? Can you enjoy the process even if you are not pleased with the outcome? As a side issue, is it possible to find the process difficult and frustrating and yet feel pleased and satisfied by the outcome?

2. A matter of interest

Ask children to prepare a short presentation for the rest of the class about something they love to do and try hard to improve in. (This could perhaps include playing video games but probably not eating sweets). If possible invite 'enthusiastic amateurs' into school to give similar talks about their hobbies or careers – a great way to foster home-school links.

3. Discussing quotes

Draw the class's attention to the quotes used throughout this book. Discuss as appropriate. What does it mean to be inspired? How are inspiration and the pleasure of writing linked? Make a list of the values or benefits of being able to write well/communicate effectively.

4. Word menus

Create 'word menus' of words and phrases that have similar meanings. These can be associated with particular pieces of writing or used in a general sense – as when we offer alternatives to the word 'said'. If the selections are written on cards they can be used as a resource to help children savour and appreciate their nuances. For example, looking back at the extract on page 29 what alternatives/additions/improvements can the class think of for –

- polished shoe
- went sprawling

- shriek of delight

- swirled up

- burst into giggles, etc.

What effect does a given alternative have on the way images are created in the imagination? For instance consider 'highly polished black leather shoe' as an alternative to 'polished shoe'.

5. Writing for pleasure

Encourage writing for the pleasure of the experience itself rather than with some outcome or finished product in mind. Ways of facilitating this include –

- Announcing a marking/grading amnesty. Tell the class that you will read a piece of their work just for enjoyment and that your comments – if children wish you to make any – will reflect what you liked about their work.

Teacher tip

You may well be aware of the 'three points of praise' rule. If not, this suggests that when marking work critically find three things to comment on positively for each corrective comment you make. For younger children use the tactic called 'three stars and a wish'.

- On other occasions mark selectively, e.g. just for punctuation or just for spelling. I have also met teachers who have invited suggestions from the children about what aspect of their work to mark and comment on. In many cases young writers show great perspicacity in knowing where there are weaknesses in their work.

     Set up a 'cooling off drawer'. Place children's work in here and leave it for a period of time; several weeks, even a whole term. Give the work back out and ask the children to notice how they could improve upon it now. Such improvements will reflect not only their further knowledge of the technical aspects of the work but are likely to reflect the children's greater sophistication now as writers – more insights into how the plot can be strengthened, characters made more believable etc. The cooling off drawer makes the 'learning curve' observable. It is a technique that many professional (read 'amateur') authors employ between drafts. 'Curve' is not really an accurate metaphor to use. Learning in whatever sense as a writer can seem more like battling over a rugged landscape! This is a more useful comparison to make, if only to suggest that 'the longest journey is tackled one step at a time.'

- All writers together. Encourage children to share their writing experiences. This will include their difficulties, frustrations and setbacks as much as their achievements. Cultivate an environment of mutual respect and support as children learn to become better writers. As often as you can, write when the children write and join in as an equal when it comes to sharing experiences. Modelling the attitude is a powerful motivator.

- Personal writing journal. Give each child a notebook that is for their use alone. In there they can put pieces of writing they don't want anyone else to see, plus their own comments about their writing 'journey'. Children can share their thoughts if they wish. Should a number of children want this, arrange time to do it properly – that is to say, without any sense of fitting it in or wanting to move on to more important things. Journal thoughts should again be shared within an atmosphere of respect and positive support.

- Book events. Many schools celebrate World Book Day and foster a tradition of inviting an author to visit. If this is not happening in your school, consider implementing something along these lines, if only on a modest scale through displays, pupil reading/storytelling sessions and so on. It doesn't take too much time or effort to create a sense of excitement around books, reading and writing. A few useful websites are:
  - ✔ www.booktrust.org.uk
  - ✔ www.contactanauthor.co.uk
  - ✔ Federation of Children's Book Groups – www.fcbg.org.uk

Teacher tip

You might well find that if there is an unpublished or recently published children's author in your area who might be pleased to visit for nothing or for just a small fee. The author benefits by publicising and selling his/her books and through the press coverage the visit generates. Your local library might have a list of contacts.

---

6. **It feels good to have an idea**

Tell the class you are about to show them a simple image (such as the one below) and ask them 'What could this be, what does it remind you of?' Ask them to notice how it feels when an idea pops into their heads. Point out that another pleasure of writing comes in the form of having lots of ideas the children can write about.

Other benefits of running this activity –

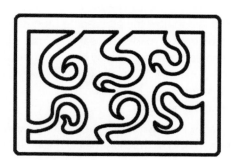

- All children experience and benefit from looking at the image in a variety of ways.
- The game emphasises the value of 'having lots of ideas in order to have your best ideas.' This is a key element of the brainstorming technique.

- The activity reinforces the ethos that the thinking of every child is valued.
- Offers a way of introducing or revisiting the 'principle of potential'. This is the notion that ideas are everywhere, but for noticing them. Even such a simple image can generate many thoughts.

Take the activity further by applying the principle of potential to more complex images. Look again at illustration on page 22 and play the 'maybe game'. Prompt the children's thinking by saying 'Maybe a flying saucer is about to land. Or maybe…?' How many maybes can the class generate?

7. Sounds good

Another pleasure to be gleaned from writing is the way words sound. By this I mean the musical alliterative quality of particular phrases and also the satisfying ongoing flow of well written sentences and paragraphs. Most Key Stage 2 children and above have learned the technical terms of alliteration, assonance, onomatopoeia etc – but I have rarely seen time given over to savouring the sound of language. A good opportunity to do this occurs when you ask children to 'turn up the sounds' during exploration of a picture (see page 22). I would make a point of saying things such as, "Oh I like that phrase you used – 'dry dusty desert' or 'birds circling slowly in the silent blue sky'". Just giving the class a few examples often prompts children to try and 'compose' similar sentences. Take it further by asking children to notice differences in sound between, say, splash and splosh or crackle and crinkle. Take it even further by the use of story readings/tellings and the reciting of poetry.

'Take a moment. Stop and think – who last touched that wall you're leaning against (great one when reaching up higher than most tourists can reach in the Roman baths in… uuhh…Bath)? How quickly could you get up that tree if a rabid dog was after you? Why is that kid shouting three streets away? How cosy would that corner be if you had to sleep rough etc? Never stop wondering.'

Gareth Mottram, author

Looking at the world

Key concept

We have already looked at the importance of observation and questioning; of being 'nosy' about the world. This section highlights the importance of children's individual perceptions and interpretations as expressed through their writing – how their particular 'take' on life is of value.

Learning benefits
- **Emphasises the value of each child's ideas.**
- **Helps to develop a sense of ownership of ideas as expressed through writing (and the oral work that may precede the writing).**

Most authors who comment on their passion for writing assert that they write primarily for themselves. In my experience it's rare to find an author who writes just for money or recognition (those that do might have a long wait!). In the classroom however, children generally write for adults; the teacher, parents, examiners. The situation is unavoidable of course and not 'wrong' as such, though I feel that the judgemental/competitive purpose behind much school-based writing needs to be tempered with the cultivation of writing purely for pleasure and for oneself. This might be achieved by devoting time to work that goes directly into children's writing journals and will be seen only by the authors themselves – see page 33.

Another ploy is to make the achievement-attainment distinction explicit (Teacher tip, page 32). I point out to young writers that there are three parts to the creation of a piece of writing. These are –

✔ Thinking time (ideas, insights, note-making).

✔ Writing time (the ongoing challenge of turning thoughts into words).

✔ Checking time. Looking back at the whole work and asking 'Can I make any changes that will help this work to be better?' and 'What have I learned by writing this that will help me to improve as a writer?' Asking these questions in actively seeking to improve means that I've worked hard to do my best. That is my achievement, whether or not the book is ever published or is successful.

This familiarises children with a key element of creative thinking, which is to look at things – experiences, ideas, arguments etc – from several viewpoints. The act of making a 'creative leap' to a new perspective draws children away from the automatic use of so-called routine thinking, which essentially means thinking about something in the same way each time. In a broad sense such a tendency can lead to (or be an expression of) a general attitude towards life. While there may be a certain 'inertia' involved in habitual thinking, unhelpful attitudes can be changed and useful attitudes reinforced.

Activities

1. Unfortunately-fortunately game

Most children enjoy this short, lighthearted activity, which makes a good warm-up to any lesson. Use a starter sentence such as 'Mr Smith was walking down the street. But unfortunately…' and invite responses. You might get: 'He was bitten by a dog.' Then you say 'He was bitten by a dog, but fortunately…' You might get: 'But it was a very little dog.' You say 'It was a very little dog, but unfortunately…' And so on.

This is one of the number of activities which leads the children to 'think unanticipated thoughts' (flipping a coin for a yes-no answer to questions is another). Within a few minutes a plot of sorts has been created which could never have been predicted. A further benefit is that all the children experience two sides to the unfolding situation. Although the 'story' itself might be frivolous, the habit of mentally flipping between two perspectives is being established, and this can subsequently become useful in more profound and important ways.

A refinement of the game is to suggest that the story must unfold within a certain genre – fantasy, spy, crime, romance etc. In this last example for instance the aggressive little dog might belong to Miss Featherdown, who hurries over to prise him loose from Mr Smith's ankle. They look into each other's eyes (Mr Smith and Miss Featherdown that is) and love blossoms from that point.

2. Perspectives jewel

Most children will have heard that 'There are two sides to every argument.' This is a partial truth because frequently issues are multi-faceted and people approach them from a wide range of viewpoints. This greater complexity can be reflected (no pun intended) by using the 'perspectives jewel'.

First select an issue. Newspapers and news websites provide plenty of choice. Create several characters (see below)– these can be stereotypes. Each character 'stands' beside a facet of the jewel and states his viewpoint. So for instance if the issue that the government wants to build a new town on greenbelt land, the characters/viewpoints in the discussion could be: oneself; local business owner; local resident; farmer who owns some of the land; unemployed person; member of a ramblers' club. The speech bubbles can be used to state the characters' basic standpoint and discussion might develop from there (although the primary purpose of the technique is to help children appreciate the multi-faceted nature of many issues, rather than to explore them in detail).

You can run the activity on a whole-class, group or individual basis. Explore the viewpoint of each character through discussion and come to an agreement about what that character might say in his or her speech bubble, including in each case a convincing reason for holding that view. This is a good opportunity to introduce 'because' as a reasoning word and for exploring the idea of stereotypes. A variation of the technique is to mark out with tape a large jewel shape in the hall and let one or more children in-role represent each character's opinion.

3. Where do I stand?

A variation of the perspectives game is to mark out a line on the floor. Select an issue such as 'Making children do homework as well as work in school time is wrong'. Ask children whether they agree or disagree and invite the two groups to stand on opposite sides of the line. Now ask each group to discuss among themselves why they hold that viewpoint and to write their reasons down on scraps of paper. Give each group scraps of a different colour. Further, ask for each reason to be rated on a 1–5 scale according to how persuasive the group feels it to be. Write the agreed number on the other side of the paper scrap and collect up the two piles of reasons, for and against.

Now instruct the groups to change places. Ask the group in favour of homework to argue against it and vice versa. Each group must now attempt to find reasons contrary to the ones they earlier discussed. Give each group scraps of two different colours from the originals. Again, a 1–5 score must be given to each reason that is marked on the other side of each scrap of paper.

You can end the activity there, as each child will have experienced considering the issue from another viewpoint. Or you can extend the game by arranging the reasons in four piles and discussing how the two piles for and the two piles against correspond, together with an assessment of the strength of the reasons.

4. If-then game

A refinement of the above activity asks children to decide where along the line they would stand (rather than on one side of it or the other). The ends of the line represent 'strongly for' and 'strongly against'. The middle of the line indicates 'undecided' or (if you allow it) 'I don't care one way or the other'.

Ask several children to position themselves along the line depending on how strongly they feel, in this case that setting homework is wrong. There's no need to ask for any reasons behind their choice if these have previously been aired.

Invite the rest of the class to work in small groups to come up with some if-then scenarios around the central topic. So –

- If the homework was limited to one day a week then...
- If I knew my test scores would improve because of homework then...
- If doing the homework always earned me house points then...
- If the homework tasks were different (decide how) from schoolwork tasks then...

Ask for some if-thens to be read out and for the children standing on the line to consider whether or not they would change their position in light of them. Arrange the activity so that all the children that want to can stand on the line, and that there are enough if-thens to allow for this.

5. If-then poems

This variation of the if-then game consolidates the activities above by flipping between upbeat and downbeat viewpoints. It also creates an opportunity to look at metaphor through poetry. Read the poem 'If Curses Were Stones' to the children.

If Curses Were Stones

If curses were stones (then)
there'd be mountains by now.

If wishes were sand
there'd be a desert by now.

If angers were raindrops
there'd be oceans by now.

If forgiveness were gold
we'd be poor by now.

This stimulus poem reflects a rather bleak outlook on life. Further lines could be added (if you really want to depress yourself) or a new version created reflecting a much more optimistic perspective. There is also an opportunity here to ask the children why they think the writer chose those particular comparisons. Would they choose different metaphors? What other emotions or qualities could be added to the piece, and what metaphors would you use to describe them?

6. If I were a spider

Another way of exploring feelings and qualities through poetry is exemplified in 'If I Were A Spider' (see below).

If I Were A Spider by Steve Bowkett

If I were a spider I'd build a web to the moon.
If I were a sound I'd be a beautiful tune.

If I were a butterfly I'd grow as big as a kite.
If I were a rainbow I'd glow and glitter all night.

If I were the sun I'd shine every day.
If I were a path I'd go the right way.

If I were a flower I'd bloom through the year.
If I were a smile I'd be full of good cheer.

If I were a thought I'd be as big as the sky.
If I were a question it would always be 'Why?'

If I were a river I'd run to the sea.
But today I think I'll just simply be me.

This poem is much more upbeat than 'If Curses Were Stones'. Again invite the children to add lines of their own or to suggest what they would do if they were spiders, sounds, butterflies, rainbows etc. What qualities do the images represent? The spider building a web to the moon represents aspiration and 'the grand vision'. What about the others? (Suitable for Key Stage 1)

Teacher tip

There isn't scope in this book to go very deeply into poetical thinking and various forms of poetry. For more information see my *Countdown To Poetry Writing* plus Sandy Brownjohn's *Does It Have To*

Rhyme?, Ted Hughes's *Poetry in the Making* and Fred Sedgewick's *Teaching Poetry*, detailed in the Bibliography.

7. How do you think he feels?

This simple technique sharpens up children's powers of observation and develops empathy. Show the class a series of pictures of different people and ask 'How do you think he or she feels?' As responses come in ask what clues the children are noticing to give them that insight? Also ask how they would describe those feelings to someone who had never experienced them (perhaps using metaphor). Look back at the characters on page 9 or show the illustration below to the class.

8. Point of view shift

You can embody some of the things the children have learned by asking them to try out some short pieces of writing. For instance:

- A complaint to a store manager about some faulty goods or bad service, and the manager's reply.
- A story extract based on fiction the children have read re-imagined in the first person from the point of view of a character other than the hero.
- How would I do it differently? Give the children a piece of text and ask them to think about how they would do it differently in terms of using alternative words/phrases/metaphors in certain cases.

Finally, as well as the learning benefits already noted for this section the activities we've looked at help children to:

- Write more perceptively in the first person (from one's own and another's perspective).
- Structure more balanced arguments.
- Detect bias more effectively, for instance in newspaper articles, readers' letters, political rhetoric etc.
- Write about characters, their motivations and relationships with greater insight.

Your imagination is all of you

'Don't tell me the moon is shining; show me the glint of light on broken glass.'

Anton Chekhov (1860–1904) Russian dramatist and physician

Key concept

Ask children to imagine sucking on a lemon and notice that some of them will make a face. It is now a well-known fact that imagining the lemon activates the same clusters of neurons in the brain that would be triggered if the lemon were actually being tasted. The same mechanism can make us frightened reading a spooky story or shiver in a different way as we read a vivid description of a winter's day. It is a phenomenon that children can exploit as they learn to think like writers.

Learning benefits

- **Raises awareness of the mind-body link.**
- **Develops metacognitive skill.**
- **Refines the senses.**
- **Serves as an ongoing resource for generating vivid details in writing.**

Activities

1. Making sense of it

Give out a piece of fruit to each child (though they might prefer sweets). Check for food allergies and intolerances beforehand. Ask them to concentrate as they look at the fruit in detail. Prompt them to notice its colours, weight, texture and smell. Squeeze the fruit slightly and notice what that feels like. Tell the children to take their time over this: the aim of the activity is to gather sensory information, so noticing small details is important. If the fruit needs peeling, again do this slowly and with concentration. Take a first taste of the fruit using the whole area of the tongue. Breathe in through the nose to heighten the taste. Chew the fruit slowly moving the morsel around the mouth. Be aware of the texture. Swallow the fruit and notice the subtleties of the aftertaste… In other words savour the experience.

It isn't necessary to do any writing at this stage, although some children might want to so you could consider allowing time for this. Normally if I do the activity in the morning I ask the children to remember their experience of eating the fruit in the afternoon. Ask them to go through the whole thing again in their imagination and if possible as slowly as when they actually ate it. Encourage them to 'mime' holding, peeling, smelling and chewing the fruit. Then ask them to write a brief description. (Suitable for Key Stage 1)

(The word remember can be read re-member and literally means 'to bring back into the members'; to recreate physically the experience that is being imagined.)

Teacher tip

Some children may not have the vocabulary to communicate the vividness of their imagined experience. In one sense (as it were) this doesn't matter as we're aiming to develop the imagination. Supply descriptive words as you feel appropriate – though the activities below will help children to be more resourceful themselves. Also make a distinction between the sensory details and the children's reactions to them. In other words if a child writes 'It had a lovely sweet taste' point out that 'sweet' describes the taste and 'lovely' describes the child's opinion of the taste.

Take the activity further by asking children to handle interesting objects like pebbles, pieces of wood etc. Get them to slowly crinkle Cellophane, listen to the sound a length of tinfoil makes when it is shaken or the noise of a marble rolled across a tabletop. Ask the class to come up with a list of sensory experiences (editing as necessary) that you can use to further develop the imagination and as a stimulus for writing.

Teacher tip

Especially in the early days of doing this kind of activity you'll have children who say things such as 'the lemon has a lemony taste'. A useful ploy is to reply 'Pretend I've never tasted a lemon. What words can you write (or say now) that would give me that lemon taste in my mouth?'

From the outset look out for greater and more vivid sensory details in the children's work. You can acknowledge their efforts by using VAK-stars in the margin – see below. In many cases overuse of a technique is part of the learning process – we all know children who sprinkle their work excessively with apostrophes after we've done a lesson on them! So there may be a glut of sensory details to begin with. Use your judgement in telling children to moderate their use.

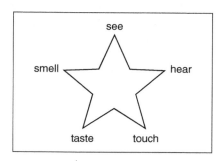

2. Sensory journey

You can extend the sensory experience by weaving a number of examples into a short narrative. So you might accompany children on 'A visit to the seaside' or 'An evening at the funfair' etc.

All you'll need to do, having chosen your topic, is to jot down a short list of things you want the children to think. For the seaside example you might ask them to imagine what it feels like to walk barefoot over shingle, or trudge through fine dry sand. Engage all the senses – the smell of the sea salty air, the cry of seagulls, the colourful swooping and whirling of kites, and so on. As before, encourage children to remember the sensory details: if you want them to pick up a pebble, tell them to hold it in their hands. If you'd like them to eat candyfloss, get them to open their mouths and take a great bite of it.

I find that telling a sensory journey in the second person works best, as it speaks directly to the listener and creates a sense of immediacy for the experience. Also toggling between past and present tense, while grammatically suspect, serves the useful purpose of heightening the here-and-now aspect of what is being imagined.

So you might say 'You have travelled by train (or whatever) to the seaside and taken a taxi to the beach. As you step out, notice the smell of the air. Take a great deep lungful of sea air… Pretend I've never smelt sea air before. Write down some words that would make me smell it now.'

At this stage pause for 30 seconds to a minute to give children time to think and write. Point out that no one has to write anything down if they choose not to. But encourage everyone to have a go. Also, avoid spoon-feeding as far as you can. Saying 'Take a great deep lungful of that fresh, warm, salty sea air' is overly prescriptive and may prevent children from having ideas and choosing words of their own.

The sensory journey can be as long or brief as you want it to be, though I do recommend a minimum of ten minutes. Progressively longer journeys develop children's ability to internalise their attention, concentrate and notice details. After you've tried out the technique a few times with your class, many children will be able (and willing) to create their own sensory journeys. There would be no need to write these out in full, just a list of things they would want their classmates to think about – so less enthusiastic writers may be tempted on board. Keep the children's notes as a resource for the future. (Suitable for Key Stage 1)

I tend to end the activity by suggesting that each child 'brings back' some small memento of the journey: a seashell they picked up on the beach, a soft toy they won at the fairground etc. I ask children to make a note of this in their writing journals.

3. 'It tastes like tinkly music'

The interaction between mind and body as we think is further reflected in the language in a fascinating way. Many words 'blur the boundaries' between the senses. Consider the following examples – austere, backbone, chewy, crisp, earthy, flabby, green, high notes, lean, sharp, silky, steely, undertones… We might recognise 'austere' as an attitude of harshness; 'backbone' as an anatomical feature or, metaphorically, referring to courage; 'green' as a colour etc. But all of the words in the list are terms used by wine connoisseurs to describe the smell and taste of wine – in fact the whole physical experience of drinking it.

On reflection this kind of sensory crossover is common. At a fairly early age we make the connection between emotions and colours. Just about every child knows that red represents anger for instance and most could work out the rationale that we actually turn red when enraged. Similarly the red for danger link may be connected with blood. Why green represents envy however is less clear (there are some interesting speculations on the internet).

- Raise children's awareness of sensory crossovers by discussing words such as soft, which refers both to texture and volume, or high, which is a spatial reference and, again, a way of describing sound.

- Extend the idea by introducing simile and metaphor. For example 'the cold wind cut like a knife' or 'the wind brushed by my legs as softly as a kitten'. Play with the language: the notion of a 'cutting' wind is commonplace, but what about a 'kittening' wind? Ask the children to pretend they are standing outdoors and to be aware of the movement of the air. Tell them to imagine a candyfloss wind, a silky wind, a sandpaper wind etc. They can write down their impressions each time, tell a partner, or simply have the experience. Subsequently, look for and encourage the use of these more original metaphors in their writing.

Teacher tip

There is an opportunity here to explore what might be called metaphorical 'themes'. I've found the following examples stimulate some interesting discussion:

- The way that time is described in terms of space (a long time ago, the distant past, putting the incident behind us etc).
- The way that intelligence is linked with light (bright, dull, brilliant – and Poincaré's moment of illumination of course).
- The way that moods and attitudes are linked with space (depressed, feeling low, I'm walking on air, things are looking up, etc).

---

4. Using metaphors in education

The metaphors used in the language of education have been touched on elsewhere. Brainstorm ideas with the class around this theme. What if we used gardening/horticultural comparisons when talking about learning (flourishing, cultivating, nurturing, seedlings, growth etc)? Or what if we used musical terms (harmony, orchestrate, chorus, chord, melody etc)? What if we compared learning to cookery (prepare, simmer, ingredients, rolling boil, blend, drizzle, fold, garnish etc)?

Teacher tip

A simpler and quicker activity is to say 'The mind is a rocket because…?' After collecting some ideas, suggest further comparisons: the mind is a spiderweb, a cloud, a symphony, a meal, a leopard, the sky – because…?

---

5. Metaphors and the senses

Use the blending of the senses to encourage descriptive writing.

- Play some instrumental music. Say to the class 'If this music were a person, what would he or she be like?'

- Look at a piece of abstract art. 'If this was a meal, what do you taste and smell? What does the food feel like as you chew it?' Or 'If this were music, what are you hearing?'

- Look at a landscape. 'If this was a person's life story, what has he or she experienced?'

'The mind is not a vessel to be filled, but a fire to be lighted.'

Plutarch (c.46–120 AD) Greek historian and biographer

5
Getting ready to write

'Talent alone cannot make a writer. There must be a man behind the book.'

Ralph Waldo Emerson (1803–1882) American essayist and poet

Be prepared

> **Key concept**
>
> Preparedness to write is not just a matter of having the right equipment or even a subject to write about. More basically it is a willingness to engage with the ongoing challenge of expressing one's thoughts in words. That's what makes writing a discipline, both in terms of 'sticking with it' and in the sense of 'learning, gaining knowledge' (from Latin *disciplina*).

Learning benefits

- **Highlights the value of determination and resilience and their link with achievement (and the satisfaction that brings).**
- **Raises awareness of the fact that writers never stop learning.**
- **Helps young writers to become more organised and systematic in their working methods.**

Activities

1. Good writing practice

Work with the class to create a poster or display of tips for writing well. This should not be about doing your best handwriting or remembering your punctuation. Rather, the emphasis is on 'what works for me' in terms of good practice. Some ideas from young writers include –

- Write on a subject you care about or that excites you.
- Try to make even boring topics interesting. Pretend it has already been written by someone else and you're reading it now and find it really interesting. How has the writer done that?
- Write regularly. A little bit of writing for pleasure every day is good.

- Take regular breaks.
- Keep your writing safe. If you use a computer, back up your work.
- Just cross out your mistakes – or 'changes of mind' – so that you can see how your thinking works.
- Never throw your work away. Look back over old writing to see how much you have improved.
- Ask yourself – what have I done well in this piece of writing? What hasn't worked so well? What else have I learned?
- Your writing represents you, so take pride in it.

2. **Beginning, middle and end**

Most children know that a piece of writing has a beginning, a middle and an end. It's important to point out to them that this is what it looks like when it's finished. The reason is that in my experience young writers feel they must get the beginning sorted out before they can tackle the rest of the piece. We teach them – rightly – that a story, newspaper article, essay etc should begin in a way that quickly interests the reader. But sometimes ideas for a 'punchy opening' emerge out of writing other portions of the work. Here are some techniques for helping children to organise their thoughts, while damping down the tendency always to begin at the beginning. (We'll use the story form as an example but the ideas apply to other forms also.)

a. When you were thinking about your story, what pictures sprang to mind (or sounds, feelings etc)? Make a note of them on sticky notes. Draw a line on a large sheet of paper. Mark the left-hand end of the line 'beginning' and the right-hand end 'end'. Can you fit any of your sticky notes on the line? You don't need to know how your story will start to do this.

Sticky notes are better than writing directly on the sheet because this allows children to reposition the notes as their overview of the story emerges. In fact you can emphasise that it's fine for children to change their minds in this way: they are not 'committing themselves to paper' in the same way as when they actually write the story.

In the context of getting ready to write, see also the section on writing for pleasure, page 33.

b. Something else you can do is place a sticky note in the middle of a blank sheet and make an ideas web around it. This means jotting down any thoughts linked to that first idea. It doesn't matter how large or small the ideas web is in the end. It also doesn't matter if you don't use all of the information eventually. The whole point of the activity is to have as many ideas as possible and to start to organise them.

c. Sparky words. These are words that spark off other ideas that will make a story more interesting. Examples are: danger, chase, threat, loss, betrayal, rescue, conflict, disguise, attack. Again you can create an ideas web for each sparky word, or use a question star and coin flips. Here's how that works:

d. Question star and coin flip. The question star encourages you to ask the big open questions: where, when, what, who, why and how. So you might ask 'Who is in danger?' Flipping a coin can only give you a yes/no answer to a closed question, so out of your open question must come one or more closed questions. So 'Is the hero in danger?'. If 'no' you might try 'Is the hero's best friend in danger?'. And so on. Once you have a 'yes' answer you can ask another 'who' question ('Who put the hero's best friend in danger?') or switch to a different question word.

If you like 'taking your mind by surprise' in this way mark your story line 1–5, where 1 is at the start. Roll a dice to find out where in the story the danger happens. You can do this with the rest of your sparky words too.

Applying the technique of actively seeking clarification develops children's critical thinking and reduces the chances of a listener misinterpreting what the speaker has said. Behind this might be the intention to show respect for the speaker's thoughts or (perhaps in the face of political rhetoric or the persuasive manipulations of advertisers) not to accept blindly what's being said.

If you are familiar with neuro-linguistic programming (NLP) you will know that such open questioning acts as a bridge between the words actually spoken (the 'surface structure' of the communication with its deletions, distortions and generalisations) and its full linguistic richness rooted in a far more complex mental network of ideas (the 'deep structure'). If NLP is new to you I recommend O'Connor and Seymour's *Introducing Neuro-Linguistic Programming*.

3. A writer's notebook

Most serious writers carry a notebook and at least one pen (by 'serious' I mean those having the earnest intention to develop as a writer, not a lack of light-hearted playfulness in learning the craft). A colleague of mine who ran a 'get children writing' project in a deprived area made sure that every child who came on the workshops was given (to keep) a stylish spiral-bound notebook and a couple of colourfully decorated pens. As in the case of the personal writing journal mentioned on page 33, these goodies came with the promise that no one would pry into any child's notebook without their consent – though many of the children were proud to show off their work. To encourage the use of a notebook further, consider the following –

- The notebook is not the same as the writing journal. A writer's notebook is there to scribble down ideas that just pop into mind, record snippets of conversation, thumbnail descriptions of people, places and things, jot down interesting words etc. These go into the notebook because they are interesting or because the writer wants to find out more. Not all of this material needs to be used in subsequent work.

- A writer's notebook is often messy. Because ideas are recorded on the spot they are often scribbled quickly with little regard for spelling, punctuation, grammar or neatness. As long as the words are legible that's OK.

    (A writer friend of mine once felt the need to scribble something in his notebook in the middle of an Iron Maiden concert, much to the puzzlement of his head-banging friends. And if you've never heard of Maiden, shame on you.)

- Suggest to young writers that they go through their notebooks occasionally to sift through what's there. Notebooks are not much use if they are not revisited and the ideas in them are unused. You might even build in some regular class time to allow children to do this.

4. Using the ideas

Notebook ideas may or may not find their way into more polished writing afterwards. However an important principle in thinking like a writer is that 'nothing is ever wasted'. Here are some ways of maximising the usefulness of the children's notes –

- Set up a 'treasure box of ideas' that any child can contribute to. Any (appropriate) idea that has been recorded in a notebook is rewritten neatly on a piece of paper and dropped into the box. It must be made clear that treasure box ideas now enter 'the public domain'. Children are free to dip into the box and either pick an idea at random or sift through to find things that either link with a project they are already attempting, or that might spark off a fresh thought or insight. (Suitable for Key Stage 1)

- A further use for the treasure box is to use its contents as the basis for mini-discussions, which occasionally have the potential to evolve into lengthier debates or even philosophical enquiries (for more information on Philosophy for Children – P4C – see page 77 and Bibliography).

Year 6 treasure box snippets

- Saw a man with piercings all over his face and he had spiky hair.

- In the supermarket there was a spray for cats called 'Silent Flea Killer', but I've never seen a noisy flea.

- It rained and our front garden smelled damp – but a nice smell. How do we decide how smells are nice or not?

- There were two girls laughing at an overweight man across the street (he was really overweight) and I thought that wasn't fair.

- Up the street from us there was a dead cat lying at the side of the road. I thought that somebody was going to be very sad.

- Let children record snippets from their notebooks on to index cards and make up themed resource boxes. These might include fragments of dialogue, descriptions of places, descriptions of people, 'seed' ideas for stories, poems, articles etc.

Teacher tip

Help get children into the habit of scribbling in the notebook by handing out optional tasks such as:

✔ Find two words you've never seen before and write them down.

✔ Jot down something that made you laugh.

✔ Record two sights, sounds etc that you found really interesting.

✔ Do a three-sentence description of a person you observe.

✔ Make a note of something you disagree with.

- Another way of keeping notebook ideas organised is for a young writer to have a separate folder or plastic slipcase for each story (or whatever) that she is working on. Often writers will have more than one project 'simmering' in their heads. If this is so for any children in the class, suggest that they use different sections of the notebook for the different things they're working on. Periodically pages are then taken out of the notebook and placed in the different project folders. Explain that a great deal of the thinking that goes into written work happens subconsciously. In order for ideas to appear 'out of the blue', material must be assimilated and new connections made at a deeper level of the mind. Much as a computer will take time to process tasks while you're still working with an open application, so too is the mind subconsciously busy on a piece of writing before, during and after it has been put down on paper.

Working in this way allows projects to grow 'organically' in children's imaginations at various rates. Obviously deadlines for some pieces of work are important and many of the techniques in this book show young writers how to develop their skills and individual pieces more quickly. However this must be balanced with a light touch when it comes to encouraging children to write for pleasure. The word 'organically' is used deliberately to reinforce the point above but also in contrast to the teaching of writing through the mechanical application of grammatical rules. In my opinion good writing (including clarity and accuracy) grows out of the creative challenge of expressing thoughts through language: experience embodied in writing for pleasure creates the best possible context for realising the importance of spelling, grammar and so on.

- Micro poems. These are little snapshots of what children observe, think and feel and have recorded in their notebooks. Some years back I devised what I called the 'myku' form (from 'my haiku). This has a 2 – 3 – 4 syllable structure over three lines. In my experience less confident or accomplished writers found them easier to create than the more complex haiku form. A selection based on things children recorded in their notebooks appears below. Once you've tried the technique out with the class you might well find that children are keen to experiment with different short forms of their own.

Cosmos,
Curlicue –
A mystery!

The cat
slides on ice –
looks so put out!

Last night –
moon through mist.
Two sights and one

So young,
fair, blue eyed –
me in mirror.

Roadside –
paper cup
just thrown away!

Getting in the mood to write

Key concept

Many writers develop a little routine or ritual that 'switches on the creative flow'.

Learning benefit

- **Enables children to gain further control of the writing process by accessing the brain states linked to the subconscious release of fresh ideas.**

Activities

Here are some pre-writing rituals I've come across –

- Read through what you wrote yesterday.
- Make sure all of your writing materials are to hand.
- Sharpen some pencils (smell the shavings). It is said that Ernest Hemingway used this trick.
- Use the same special pencil or pen when you write for pleasure.
- Write in the same place/at the same time if you can. This works for me anyway. A writer friend of mine however is so nervous about 'getting writer's block' at an established location that he deliberately writes in different places to reduce the chances of his mind 'seizing up'.
- Play the same piece of music each time before you settle to write.
- Deliberately relax, slow your breathing and look forward to the fresh thoughts you can write about today.
- Make sure the house is clean and neat (you might not be able to get children to tidy your classroom though).

What all of these techniques have in common is that they create and strengthen an association between a chosen stimulus and the (pleasurable) act of writing. In NLP terms (see page 48 and Bibliography) this is known as anchoring. An anchor is a link that is made between a particular behaviour and a sight, sound, object etc that you have under conscious control. A stimulus need not be external, but could be a mental image, the recollection of a sound or object.

It's important, I feel, for each child to choose an anchor for him/herself once the idea has been explained. But you can begin to establish 'anchors for writing' across the whole class before introducing the idea: in this case the process will be working subconsciously as far as the children are concerned.

For instance, and if possible, you might ask children to look through their notebooks or put something in their writing journals at a particular time in the day. Or, at least, you can stand in the same place whenever you talk about writing, offer tips and advice, invite children to read their work etc. In this case you will be creating a spatial anchor where children (again usually subconsciously) come to associate you being at that spot with the enjoyment of writing and writing-related activities.

Incidentally, spatial anchoring is an elegant technique for managing the class in different ways. You might establish an anchor spot for introducing new ideas and knowledge and another spot when you want children to recall information. Try standing in the same place each time when you need to admonish or otherwise administer discipline. In one classroom where I was working both the teacher and I noticed two boys talking to one another and not paying attention to what she was saying. Without even breaking the flow of her conversation she began to move towards what she called her 'telling off spot'. Before she even reached it the two boys were facing front paying attention. If you think it's coincidence, try it for yourself – you've got nothing to lose.

In this case of course you don't tell the children about the anchor point, but when you want them to establish personal anchors for writing they will need to understand the idea of anchoring. My own trick for getting in the mood to write is to read through the last five pages I've written. I also have a small glass paperweight nearby which I hold whenever I need to pause in the work to reread something or compose the next few sentences. This simple device works very well for me.

The confidence to try

'It is not because things are difficult that we do not dare; it is because we do not dare that they are difficult.'

Seneca (4 BC – 65 AD) Roman philosopher and dramatist

Key concept

A very close link exists between creativity, effective thinking and a degree of self-confidence and increasing self-esteem in children. Pursuing a 'thinking agenda' in your classroom necessarily means working to develop the willingness to try in young writers.

Learning benefits

- **Offers an alternative to the competitive-judgemental ethos that usually exists within a system driven by results.**
- **Implicitly allows children to understand that writing for pleasure rests on a platform of values different from those that often drive people in society (wealth, fame, power).**
- **Helps children to become more emotionally resourceful, initially within the context of 'thinking like writers' but ultimately more broadly in their lives.**

The 'what could this be?' game in 'It feels good to have an idea' on page 34 is one technique among many that helps children to understand the ethos that underpins the aim of helping them to think like writers. In summary this is –

- All children are entitled to become more independent thinkers.
- Ideas should be valued for themselves (refining them, strengthening them and assessing their usefulness comes later).
- Mistakes and 'doing it wrong' indicate emergent understanding and are opportunities for further learning. (A classic example I came across recently was the young child who said 'Yesterday I wented to the shops.' Do we simply correct the sentence or also recognise it as the emergent understanding of the grammatical structure of the past tense?)
- Asking (especially open) questions is an intelligent behaviour that signifies 'I want to learn more'. That should be the emphasis rather than 'I'm ignorant because I don't know'.

- Striving towards personal betterment is more important than trying to outdo others.
- Writing well, and for pleasure, is an end in itself. The journey is the destination – see The hero's journey on page 60.

Activities

1. The 'zone cone'

Use a version of the diagram below to help children assess what they can do easily and what they find more difficult. Link it with the idea that always staying within what has come to be called the 'comfort zone' does not usually help to develop one's full potential. Carol Dweck in *Self-Theories* (see Bibliography) points out that there is a tendency among some 'bright' children to go for the easier option because they are more likely to succeed at the task and therefore maintain their higher status. An even worse case scenario exists when children who are convinced (i.e. have developed a self-theory) that they will fail don't even try.

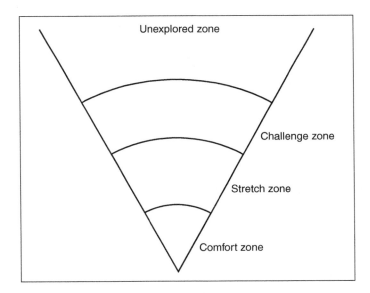

Reproduce the zone cone onto A4 sheets and ask the children to write something in each section.

- In the 'comfort zone' make a note of at least one thing you know you do because it's easy (even if you feel good when you do it well). On 12 September 1962 U.S. President John F. Kennedy made his famous speech at the Rice University Stadium where, for the sake of national pride, he committed America to putting a man on the Moon and bringing him safely back to Earth before the decade was out. We choose to do these things, Kennedy said, not because they are easy but because they are hard. For me it is one of the most powerful and moving speeches I have ever heard (http://er.jsc.nasa.gov/seh/ricetalk.htm). It is all the more poignant in light of Kennedy's assassination just over a year later; all the more wonderful when Neil Armstrong set foot on the Moon within six months of JFK's deadline.

- In the 'stretch zone': note something that maybe you have to struggle with but you try anyway, even if you fail, because you want to master it. 'Stretching' is a metaphor commonly used in education along with pushing, pulling, keeping up, falling behind, slipping back etc. It is language rooted in competitiveness – see the note on metaphors (page 44). I think it is valuable to take time discussing this with the class, emphasising that 'failure' (or 'not having succeeded yet') is part of the learning process. A Chinese proverb puts the idea into perspective – 'Failure is not in falling down but in refusing to get back up.' Another useful source of insight is to be found in Thomas Edison the scientist/inventor whose attitude towards failure is inspirational. Among other things he said 'I've failed my way to success'. Edison patented 1,093 inventions, more than any other inventor in history (http://bigthink.com/ideas/16667).

- In the 'real challenge zone' write something that, at the moment, you haven't attempted because you think you won't be able to do it (but maybe you'll give it a go).

- The 'unexplored zone' contains all the help, skills and knowledge out there to help you to achieve your goals. Maybe your teacher and other students would write something in that part of the cone; something that they learned, something they achieved, maybe something they have yet to master.

2. Inspirational quotes and posters

Hundreds of such quotes are to be found online, while many classrooms I've visited feature them (including, alas, curled and yellowing photocopies of sayings stuck high up on the wall where children cannot read them). Inspiration is a powerful and necessary element of thinking like a writer of course (pages 5–6), though I qualify my own use of such material in two ways –

- beware overkill
- be realistic.

Too much inspirational/motivational material in my opinion simply desensitises. Posters displayed everywhere or for long periods simply become invisible. I'm also a little sceptical of the 'anybody can achieve anything if they try hard enough' school of thought. I believe that effort and determination offer a person the greatest chance of fulfilling his potential in a chosen field but that (due to the complex interweaving of nature and nurture) such potential is not unlimited. When I talk to children about this I emphasise that I love writing and work hard to do my best, but that there will always be more talented and successful authors out there. For me that attitude highlights the distinction between personal achievement and externally judged attainment – i.e. I feel a great sense of satisfaction and fulfilment in finishing a book: if it's published, that's a bonus. If it does well, that's another bonus.

Here are some ideas for working with motivational material –

- Tell the class from time to time about people in different fields who achieved success through their own endeavours – or invite children to do some research for themselves. The activity makes for a useful five-minute filler and over time raises awareness of qualities common to the individuals concerned.

- Draw up a list of such qualities – determination, dealing with disappointment, self-belief etc – and make a class poster prominently displayed.

Rejections

Many aspiring authors take comfort in the fact that a large number of highly successful writers endured a long and difficult 'apprenticeship' when their work was repeatedly rejected before it was recognised. Among them are:

The Diary of Anne Frank rejected 16 times.

Dubliners by James Joyce, rejected 22 times.

Gone With the Wind by Margaret Mitchell, rejected 38 times.

Animal Farm by George Orwell, rejected three times, including once by the poet T. S. Eliot who was an editor with Faber & Faber at the time.

Harry Potter book one by J. K. Rowling, rejected nine times, I'll bet they're kicking themselves!

Teacher tip

Discussing how to handle rejection and related issues, combined with developing emotional resourcefulness in children more generally, takes on an added importance when the time comes for them to apply for university places, jobs and so on.

---

3. Writing buddies

I have been in several schools where more skilled writers mentor the less experienced, or at least volunteer to sit and chat with a young writer and take an interest in their work. The scheme works particularly well if the two children are interested in the same topics or genres for writing. For instance, at one school some Year 9 boys who ran a fantasy role play club visited Year 7 English classes to talk about their interest and subsequently helped some of the pupils to develop their own fantasy stories. The older students' enthusiasm for their hobby was at least as valuable as the technical details they supplied.

4. Coaching conversations

Coaching is different from mentoring in so far as the coach does not offer advice but, through careful listening and asking appropriate questions enables the 'coachee' to reflect on the matter to be resolved and make necessary decisions to achieve the desired goal.

Children would need to practise a number of techniques to be able to take part in a useful coaching conversation, but the skills are not difficult to learn and bring broader educational benefits.

Peer coaching

A typical peer-coaching conversation in the context of solving a problem in writing might look like this:

Coach: What do you want to achieve?
Coachee: I don't know how to start my story.

Coach:	That's the problem, but what do you want to achieve?
Coachee:	I want to write a really good opening to my story.
Coach:	OK, so what does 'really good' mean to you?
Coachee:	Interesting, exciting, so the reader gets involved.
Coach:	Do you already know some of the things you'll put in your story?
Coachee:	Yes.
Coach:	Good. And are some of them exciting and interesting?
Coachee:	Yes.
Coach:	What makes them like that?
Coachee:	Well, there's action. And I use short sentences and strong verbs.
Coach:	What else?
Coachee:	I mention colours and sounds and smells, and how the characters are feeling.
Coach:	So how will that help?
Coachee:	I could put the same things into the start of my story.
Coach:	So you'll open your story by using short sentences, strong verbs and you'll describe sights, sounds, smells and how the characters are feeling?
Coachee:	Yes.
Coach:	What will you do to begin achieving that?
Coachee:	Think about my opening scene and imagine colours and sounds.
Coach:	What else?
Coachee:	I'll make notes about that and get a better idea of what my characters look like.
Coach:	When will you do that?
Coachee:	In writing time today…

5. Wheel of writing

A well-known tool in coaching sessions is the 'wheel of life'. Here a circle is divided into a number of areas and these are then filled in to indicate the amount of time devoted to them, the degree to which they bring fulfilment etc. Typically in life coaching the segments will be labelled work, mother/father, husband/wife, hobbies, money, holiday and so on. The wheel aims to provide a graphic representation of any areas of life that are out of balance.

A variation of the idea can be used to help children 'balance up' their writing skills. Suggested labels for segments appear in the diagram opposite, but children can choose their own individually or through group/class discussion. Each section will clearly show areas where a child struggles or worries and also aspects of the writing that are going well and being tackled with confidence. Coaching conversations might throw up insights for resolving areas of difficulty. Alternatively a child achieving highly in one area can become the writing buddy of a classmate struggling with the same aspect of writing. The wheels also provide a snapshot of a child's progress if the activity is run several times through the year.

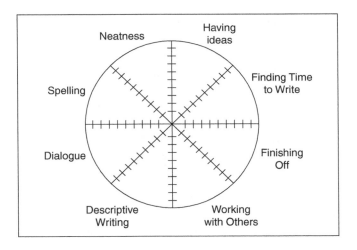

'Make the most of yourself, for that is all there is of you.'

Ralph Waldo Emerson, American poet and essayist

The hero's journey

'Books are those faithful mirrors that reflect to our mind the minds of sages and heroes.'

Edward Gibbon (1737–1794) English historian

In traditional tales particularly the basic structure of a narrative looks like this.

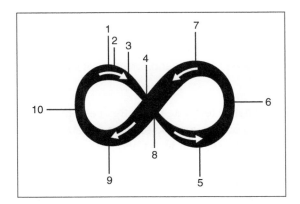

(This image first appeared in *Developing Literacy and Creative Writing Through Storymaking* by Steve Bowkett © 2010, reproduced with the kind permission of Open University Press. All rights reserved.)

The left hand lobe represents our ordinary lives and day-to-day experiences while the right hand side is 'the unknown realm' of new challenges where the hero's mettle is tested, dangers are faced, villainy is overcome and the central problem resolved so that harmony and balance can be restored to the world.

There are ten significant points along the roller-coaster path of the hero's journey. These are –

1   A call to action. A problem arises but at first the hero is reluctant to become involved. Life is just too comfortable!

2   Heeding the call. Realising that things can't remain as they are and, through loyalty to others and a sense of duty, the hero commits him or herself to action and sets off along the path.

3   An initial challenge brings the hero's first brush with adversity. Imagining the image as a roller-coaster we see that the hero is already plunging down towards greater dangers and difficulties.

4   Passing beyond the threshold provides a major crisis for the hero. In traditional stories a 'threshold guardian' often appears here to test the hero's noble qualities. The guardian might be a character in the story, but could just as well be some element of the hero's own psyche. (The origin of 'crisis' is the Greek krinein meaning 'to sift, separate, judge, decide', from keirein, 'to cut'. Interestingly the root is shared by 'certain' and 'critic'.)

5   This is often called 'the point of lowest ebb' where difficulties can seem insurmountable. The hero is, as it were, deep in alien territory and forced to rely on her own resources. Recognising these strengths begins to lift the hero out of despair. Things seem to be looking up.

6   Here the hero is as far from home as she can be and here faces her greatest test.

7   After struggle comes success. But it's easy to grow complacent or to think that the problem has been solved, whereas in fact there is a further descent into danger and more challenges follow.

8   However the hero has shown determination, resilience, judgement and courage; and although the same or another threshold guardian puts a further obstacle in the hero's way she is heading home (though is not on the home straight).

9   A final crisis follows, a twist in the tale that keeps the story interesting but also allows the hero to realise that even here on home ground she can't afford to rest on her laurels.

10 The most satisfying ending sees all the present challenges met and the current problem resolved. The hero brings home well earned rewards and, for a time at least, restores harmony and balance to her world.

Significantly the shape of the narrative template is also the mathematical sign for infinity. In human life there will always be villainy and problems to solve so there will always be the need for heroism. This is why stories feature a resolution, a 're-solution' to yet another variation on situations that are as old as humankind.

Used as a plotting device the narrative template offers flexibility within a robust structure. It is more elegant and sophisticated than the narrative line we looked at on page 48. Further uses for the template appear in *Developing Literacy and Creative Writing Through Storymaking*, but you might introduce it to the class now in these ways –

1. The hero's journey

Use the template to map out key events in a book or film you are studying with a class. The writer Stuart Voytilla in his book *Myth and the Movies* did just this with 50 of the most memorable movies of the twentieth century and discovered that they shared basic mythic elements and by and large followed the pattern of the narrative template above.

2. Statements grid

Choose a number between 1 and 6. Roll a dice to select a box from the grid below. You'll notice that the statements are deliberately vague (flexibility within a structure again). Use coin flips to explore the chosen statement and flesh out that part of the story. The technique is useful for generating a storyline from scratch, learning more about key events and making progress if a child gets stuck at any point.

	1	2	3	4	5	6
1	Consider your needs.	Partnerships are likely.	Look for signals.	Time to separate.	Unexpected help appears.	Be strong in a new way.
2	Go into new areas.	Choose carefully.	Treasures are all around.	Look to your defences.	An arrival is both good and bad.	Protect yourself.
3	Some object becomes important.	Something useful is found.	Your plans bring rewards.	A way opens up to you.	Something once lost is now found.	Fight for what you want.
4	Now is a time of growth.	Remove an obstacle.	Go with the flow.	Plans are upset.	A coincidence helps you.	Important messages due.
5	The landscape is to your advantage.	Choose the opposite.	What was two is now united.	Time to trust in another.	What you say now is vital.	Beware a clever trap.
6	You are on a threshold.	There is a break-through.	Patience brings reward.	Time to change direction.	You notice a helpful sign.	A secret and the unknown.

3. Ambiguous language

Also use the grid to point out the nature of vague or ambiguous language. In the activity above we want to teach children to interpret the statements within the context of their own particular story. Sometimes however, vague statements are deliberately evasive or serve as pseudo explanations – consider the classic 'Lessons have been learned and procedures have been put in place'. In this case further questioning – the use of the question star (page 42) and the questioning technique (page 49) – immediately highlights the shortcomings of what was said and actively seeks to elicit more and clearer information.

4. The writing journey

Finally the narrative template serves well as a metaphor for the writer's own 'journey'. Although the word has become a cliché (thanks in part to its overuse on reality TV shows) it still means 'a transformative experience'. To do something because it is hard, to go into the challenge zone and tackle what you find there using your own resources will lead to the resolution of problems, the recognition of noble qualities and the bringing home of rewards in the form of new skills and a fulfilling sense of achievement.

Teacher tip

The education consultant Mike Tilling in his book *Adventures in Learning* explores the relationship between narrative structures and the personal 'stories' of individual learners, with particular emphasis on the basic narrative template and the learner's journey. Highly recommended – see Bibliography.

6
Writing techniques

Fiction, non-fiction, facts and truth

'It's no wonder that truth is stranger than fiction. Fiction has to make sense.'

Mark Twain [Samuel Langhorne Clemens] (1835–1910)
American author and humorist

Key concept

The idea that fiction comprises stories that are made up and that non-fiction consists of facts that are true is a rather naïve belief, but one that is held even by older and more sophisticated students. This chapter aims to consolidate some of the techniques in the previous section to explore the notions of fiction and non-fiction and their relationship to what is true (as far as that can be achieved). The writer Tom Clancy noted that an important difference between fiction and reality is that fiction has to make sense.

Learning benefits

- **Allows children to realise that stories, poems and other fictional forms can 'tell you something true'.**
- **Dampens the tendency for learners to be the passive and unquestioning recipients of facts.**
- **Offers techniques for assessing the veracity of factual information presented to them.**
- **Reinforces the 'think like a writer' ethos of actively seeking further details and understanding.**

Activities

1. Fiction and non-fiction

Explore the idea of fiction and non-fiction by asking the class some or all of these questions:

- What is fiction?
- What is non-fiction?

- Does non-fiction mean the same as facts? If 'yes' then what is a fact (without saying 'It is non-fiction'). If 'no' what are the differences do you think between non-fiction and facts?
- Can you think of any facts that might not be true one day?
- Can you think of any facts that, as far as we know, will always be true?
- Is the statement 'I like orange juice' true?
- If you asked me 'Steve Bowkett do you like orange juice?' and I said 'Yes', would the statement 'I like orange juice' be truer than before?
- Do you think that some facts are more important than others are (if 'yes' give examples or explain a bit more about what you mean)?
- Can a fact ever be partly true (again, give examples if you can)?
- What do you think the word 'opinion' means?
- Are some people's opinions worth more than others'?

This is an opportunity to remind the class of the value of 'it depends' (or contingent) thinking. If any child says without prompting ' It depends what you mean by "worth" or 'What do you mean by "more"?' he or she deserves a merit point.

- Is a fact the same as a reason?
- Can a reason also be an opinion?
- In what ways can an opinion be true?

Word roots

I wonder if like me you find the etymology of these words fascinating:

- Fact, from Latin facere 'to make'. The root is also shared by 'factory' and 'manufacture'.
- Fiction, again from Latin – fingere 'to shape, fashion, feign'.
- Opinion, via Old French from Latin opinio 'belief', from opinari 'to think'.
- Real, from Latin realis 'relating to things', akin to Sanskrit rai 'property' (as in 'real estate').
- Reason, from Latin ration – ratio 'compute': akin to Gothic garathjan 'to count, Greek arariskein 'to fit'.
- True, from Old English treowe 'loyal, trusty, honest'. Words sharing the same root are treaty, troth, truce.

Sources: *Longman Dictionary of Word Origins* / Dictionary.com.

Teacher tip

Considering questions such as those in 1. brings immediate benefits when it comes to writing argumentative essays, having debates and philosophical enquiries. Taking time to ponder the notion of facts also helps children to ask more incisive and searching questions in other subject areas.

2. Letter to the Editor

The letter below was written by Mr Albert Hall to the Kenniston Evening Gazette complaining about the introduction of car parking charges by the town council.

Albert Hall 23
Gleneagle Villas
Mannamead
Kenniston
KS3 5HJ

8th December 2014

Dear Sirs,

I read with great dismay your article of last Thursday, December 1st, reporting that the town council is planning to introduce car-parking charges in Kenniston. This is outrageous and goes against the wishes of most of the people who live here. I know the council moans about how short of money it is, but surely there are other and better ways of finding extra funds?

I wonder if our esteemed councillors have thought about who will have to bear the brunt of their ill-considered move to rip-off the people of Kenniston yet again? Have they not thought about families on low incomes or benefits who will somehow have to scrape together even more of their hard-earned cash, only to see it squandered on further impractical schemes – like last year's ridiculous Arts Festival. What did we get for our money? Clowns and people walking about on stilts! Street poets (and their poetry didn't rhyme!!) plus dreadful jazz musicians who by rights should be looking hard to find a proper job.

Not only that. What about the cost to local businesses? The Small Business Association for this region has warned that shops in the town will lose trade, since folks will shop elsewhere, such as in Clayton for instance where you can park for free. And what about people in nearby villages who don't drive? The bus service into Kenniston has been getting worse for years. Many of those who come to town each day commute by train into the city – they won't bother to pay these outlandish parking charges. Instead, obviously, they'll just leave their vehicles on side streets and clog them up for ordinary respectable townsfolk going about their day to day business.

And what about the children? Will parents driving their kids to school also have to pay? Education is important: parents have the right to choose the best schools. Therefore they should not be penalised for picking a school in Kenniston.

Finally I want to say that even if the parking fees seem 'reasonable' it is the thin end of the wedge – charges will go up in real terms year by year. No wonder thousands of people a year leave Britain and emigrate to Australia. Ours used to be a land that was the envy of the world for its fairness and honesty and for the marvellous opportunities it presented. Alas, all of that is gone now. Bringing in car parking charges is just another nail in the coffin as far as I'm concerned!!!

Yours Angrily,
Albert Hall.

---

a. Pick three statements from the letter that you think express an opinion.

b. Pick three statements that you think are facts.

c. Use the 'it depends' tool as you look at the letter. Are there any places where you could say 'It depends what you mean by…'?

d. Use the question star and make a list of some open questions that you could ask Mr Hall if you had the chance.

e. Albert Hall is obviously opposed to car parking charges in his town. What reasons does he give to support his view? Once you have found some, put them in order of how 'strong' or persuasive you think the reasons are. Think about whether the strongest reasons are supported by facts, opinions or both. Does the fact that Mr Hall feels very strongly about this matter make his case any more convincing?

f. Working in a group or as a whole class, come up with some reasons in favour of the introduction of car parking charges in the town. Put your strongest reasons/arguments at the top of your list.

g. Play a game called 'on the other hand'. Find a point that Mr Hall makes to support his view that car-parking charges are 'bad' and use the same point to suggest how car-parking charges could be good. For example –

- Mr Hall's point – Low-income families will find it harder to manage. On the other hand – This is an opportunity to cut out journeys that aren't necessary and/or to 'save up' things that need to be done in town and attend to them all during the one trip. Also it gives everyone, low income or not, a chance to look again at their priorities and values.

- Mr Hall's point – Businesses in Kenniston may lose trade if people shop elsewhere. On the other hand – The increased competition might make shops in Kenniston lower their prices or launch more special offers, attracting more shoppers.

This activity is similar to the Fortunately-unfortunately game on page 36. It is not necessary to take one side or the other in terms of what you personally believe, but simply to look at two different points of view.

h. Mr Hall uses several 'tricks' or devices to try and make his case stronger. Look for at least one example of each –

- Uses strong 'emotional' words, words that express his strong feelings.
- Claims to know what other people believe or think.
- Suggests that something should be obvious to everyone when maybe it isn't (look for '-ly' adverbs').
- Asks questions for effect rather than because he expects an answer (rhetorical questions).
- States facts without evidence or proof.
- Uses comparisons (metaphors) to try and influence how you feel.

i. Imagine you are a spokesperson for Kenniston Council. Write a response to Mr Hall's letter stating the council's case. You can either try and write a considered, balanced and reasonable reply or one that uses the same tricks that Mr Hall does to try and win support.

j. By the way, when you were reading Mr Hall's letter did you have a picture of him in your head, or imagine him speaking? Write down your impression and compare notes with your friends.

Looking at information

'Be careful about reading health books. You may die of a misprint.'

Mark Twain

The main messages of this book, in this context, are –

- If you are writing a factual piece, check your facts, support opinions by strong reasons and if you are going to use any persuasive techniques use them deliberately.
- If you are reading factual information keep your wits about you in just the same way. The three-step questioning (page 19) is very useful in helping you to be aware of yourself and how you are reacting to the information. In terms of 'what do I need to ask to find our more' here are some handy questions –
  - What words/ideas don't I understand? (How can I find out what they mean?).
  - How recent is the information? (Where can I find more up-to-date information?).
  - Who is the author and how is he or she qualified to write these things?
  - Where else can I check these facts? (How will I know when I can accept them?).
  - Is the author trying to influence my opinion in any way? (If so how is he or she doing that?).
  - Is the information actually useful for my purpose?

Telling you something true

Learning benefits

- **Helps children to revise their definition of fiction.**
- **Encourages an active search for the truths contained in some stories, poems and other fictional forms.**
- **Paves the way for the children themselves to tell their readers something true in their own fiction.**
- **Develops a greater understanding of parable, allegory, myth and legend.**

Activities

1. Telling you something true

Look at this story below.

'Once upon a time in ancient China there lived a man called Dojen. His life was a simple one. He wandered from village to village and enjoyed watching the wonders of nature. Perhaps because his mind was uncomplicated and he saw things with a childlike eye he had a reputation for being very wise.

At that time the province through which Dojen passed was suffering many difficulties. Food was scarce, hostile tribes were threatening to invade from the north and the spring rains were overdue. The people were unhappy and worried.

The ruler of the province, M'at-su, was equally concerned. He happened to hear that Dojen was in the area and decided to seek the wise man's advice. He sent messengers to ask Dojen to meet him at a local teashop. Dojen agreed and was already there waiting when the ruler and his bodyguard appeared.

Out of respect Dojen had not sat down or ordered anything to eat or drink. But now M'at-su bade Dojen be seated and asked the teashop owner to provide the best food and drink that he had.

Soon the tea things arrived. As Dojen lifted the teapot to pour, M'at-su said, 'Now Dojen I think what we ought to do is increase taxes. The people are short of food but not money. I could use the revenue both to buy provisions from the rulers to the south and with what's left could perhaps persuade the northern tribes to look elsewhere for new lands to conquer. I also think that if the people worked harder and longer then we could…'

As M'at-su chattered on Dojen filled his cup to the brim – and kept pouring so that the tea spilled out on to the saucer. M'at-su stopped in mid-sentence and his mouth hung open in disbelief. Never had anyone shown him such disrespect. He was about to lose his temper when Dojen put the teapot down and smiled in a kindly way.

'M'at-su, you asked for my advice. But like this cup you are too full of your own opinions. When you have emptied yourself of them I will be happy to tell you what I think.'

Upon hearing this, M'at-su felt huge gratitude to wise old Dojen.

---

a. This section is called 'Telling you something true'. Do you think the story of Dojen does that? If so, what do you think it is and in what sense is it true?

b. If I told you I invented the ruler M'at-su and that he never really existed, do you think that makes the story less true?

The story uses a metaphor to make its point – the teacup was too full just as M'at-su was too full of his own opinions. Metaphors and similes are useful because they take a difficult or abstract idea and help you to imagine it as a story or a picture in your mind. An anonymous wit when asked to define a metaphor said 'A metaphor is like a simile'.

2. Playing with proverbs

Proverbs are often metaphors that aim to tell you something true. What are these examples trying to tell you that's true?

- A bird in the hand is worth two in the bush.
- A rolling stone gathers no moss.
- A stitch in time saves nine.
- Barking dogs seldom bite.
- Cut your coat according to your cloth.
- Follow the river and you will find the sea.

3. Always, never, sometimes, it depends

Having thought about the 'message' contained in these proverbs, pick one and consider whether it is always true or sometimes true (and in what circumstances), or whether the truth depends on other things – and if so, what?

Note: One function of science fiction is to hold up a mirror to society to highlight religious, political, moral issues in fresh new ways. For example H. G. Wells's *The Time Machine* is an allegorical cautionary tale about the potentially dangerous social divisions that existed in late Victorian England between the privileged upper class and the poverty stricken working masses. If you are interested in using science fiction to explore issues that are just as pertinent in today's world I recommend Mark Rowland's *The Philosopher At The End Of The Universe*.

4. Ways of looking

You may recall that in my opinion one important element of creative thinking is to take a multiple perspective on the ideas, people and events we meet in our lives; in other words to try and look at things in lots of different ways. One value of this is that we don't get locked into looking at the world from the same viewpoint – our own.

In one sense, of course, we can't help but see through our own eyes and make sense of life through the filter of our individual experiences. On the other hand, whenever we read a book, watch a movie, study a painting or listen to music, we enrich our own thinking by being exposed to someone else's outlook. Appreciating this helps us to understand that the 'many perspectives' idea operates at various levels. It's (hopefully) not controversial to say that a pessimist will look at the world differently to an optimist – or in other words and as the saying goes, 'an angry man lives in an angry world'. Perhaps more discussion would arise from suggesting that science amounts to one way of looking at existence and that religion constitutes at its heart a different but equally 'true' way of understanding ourselves within the universe.

It is beyond the scope of this book to explore the notion of the relativity (indeed the very meaning) of 'truth', but the basic point can be understood by most children and used in a practical way to help them appreciate that –

- Because we are all unique each of us has our own story to tell.

- Other people's stories (viewpoints) make our own experience richer.

- A poem, a story, a painting, a sculpture etc all represent 'ways of looking' and are most powerful when they help us to understand how other people experiences life.

- We can become more aware of someone else's viewpoint without having to agree or disagree with it.

Activities

1. Department store

Look back at the illustration on page 27 and imagine what thoughts would go through the mind of – a pickpocket/an alien/a homeless person/the store manager/someone your age.

2. Three ways of looking

Pick an ordinary object or animal or feature of the landscape. Write three sentences describing it from three different viewpoints. If you have tried the 'myku' activity on page 51 you might want to record your thoughts in the form of three 'micro poems'.

For example: A church bell striking midnight from the point of view of –

A vampire…
Waking,
feel the blood
sing in the veins.

A child lying awake…
Dark, but
no monsters
under the bed!

A prowling cat…
Shadows,
Grass, trees, stars –
This is my world!

3. Point of view

Think about a story you've enjoyed and write a short scene from the viewpoint of the villain/a minor character/a new character that you have invented (see page 9 for tips on creating characters).

Write what you know

'When you know a thing, to hold that you know it, and when you do not know a thing, to allow that you do not know it – this is knowledge.'

Confucius (551–479 BC) Chinese teacher and philosopher

Key concept

Exploring wider themes in our lives allows us to write 'what we know' at that deeper level.

Learning benefits
- **Helps children to understand the deep structure of some fiction.**
- **Develops the ability to connect the small details of experience to an overview of life.**
- **Primes children actively to question what 'knowing' means.**
- **Emphasises the value of experience and underpins the idea that experience isn't just what happens to us, but what we make of what happens to us.**

'Write what you know' is a standard piece of advice that more proficient authors often give to aspiring writers. In the activity above the children were invited to look at the world through the eyes of a pickpocket, an alien etc. So is there not a contradiction here?

It depends what you mean by 'know'. If we could (or were advised to) write only what we had directly experienced then many of us would not be able to write very much at all that was original and fresh (notwithstanding that potentially each of us sees the world in a unique way). One function of the imagination is to allow us as it were to 'stand where we have not stood before' – in other words to pretend that we could witness or be these people or creatures or whatever. The word 'pretend' comes from Latin (not surprisingly) and is pre + tendere, 'to stretch'. A vestige of this root appears in the phrase 'by no stretch of the imagination.' To pretend means to stretch or reach out with our thoughts and create scenarios that we have not actually experienced for ourselves.

Another point to make, concerns the level at which we 'know' something. In a story I wrote once a group of boys raid an old man's allotment and steal some of his fruit. Naturally they are found out. Later Mr Jones turns up at each of their homes and gives them a bag of his fruit. They reciprocate by returning to his allotment to help him dig over the ground. In fact, I was one of those boys (long ago), but out of that quite ordinary event arise some deeper 'knowings' – that events have consequences/that an individual might behave differently when in a group/that kindness can teach a more powerful lesson than punishment.

As a writer I can now take what I learned and use it in other fictional (and non-fictional) contexts. I have never been to prison (fingers crossed) but based on my understanding that kindness can teach a more powerful lesson than punishment, I could perhaps write a more insightful story than if I had never stolen Mr Jones's apples. Research into prison life would add a further dimension to the tale.

Another theme to come out of the allotment adventure is that of 'crossing the line'; the notion of stepping over a threshold into new, challenging and perhaps dangerous circumstances. If you accept the model of the basic narrative template (page 57) then it is a theme that is common to most of us and, therefore, to most stories.

We might imagine basic human themes as the roots of a vast tree and our own lives as the branches. Ordinary events connect us to our kind and in a very important way make us all participants in the greatest human adventures. While this might sound rather grandiose it brings the very practical benefit of being another source of inspiration that connects us to the world of story. That is to say, it provides a direct line between even the most exotic, fantastical tales and our day-to-day lives. And it's a two-way street. The ordinary things that happen to us offer up themes that we can explore in all kinds of ways in our writing.

Activities

1. Gathering memories

Ask the children to remember one or more events that stick in their minds, things that have happened to them which taught them a lesson in some way. These can be quite small and ordinary happenings (though the implication is that they are significant because they ring in the memory). Here are some from a class that tried the activity.

- I tried to be nice to our neighbour's cat – I stroked it and wanted to play – but it bit me. I'll try again tomorrow though.
- I broke my brother's toy car because he wouldn't let me play with it.
- Our group decided not to talk to Jane because she wore glasses.
- Even though I didn't share my sweets with Alex he offered me one of his.
- Once I stole a pencil from a shop. Nobody ever found out but I still feel bad about it.

Make it clear that the children are free to write these memories in their journals and do not need to share them. Now ask children to write beside each recollection what lesson they think they have learned from it, or at least what feelings they experienced at the time.

2. Gathering experiences

Finally, working in groups or as a whole class with the memories that have been made public, what broader themes can be distilled from them? Create a chart like the one below.

Experience	Feelings Remembered / Lesson Learned	Broader Theme(s)
I tried to be nice to our neighbour's cat – I stroked it and wanted to play – but it bit me. I'll try again tomorrow though.	Sometimes trying to be nice doesn't work. I felt annoyed and hurt.	If at first you don't succeed.

I broke my brother's toy car because he wouldn't let me play with it.	I knew I was doing wrong and being mean.	If I can't have it nobody will. Life is about the choices we make.
Our group decided not to talk to Jane because she wore glasses.	Hurt, angry. I learned that sometimes people can be spiteful for no reason.	Life happens!
Even though I didn't share my sweets with Alex he offered me one of his.	I suppose I felt kind of guilty. I decided to share my sweets next time.	Kindness is bigger than selfishness.
Once I stole a pencil from a shop. Nobody ever found out but I still feel bad about it.	Nervous and excited at the time. Guilty feelings afterwards.	You can't run away from your conscience. You can't change the past but you can change yourself.

3. What if?

You can also work it the other way round. Suggest some themes and ask the children to recall any experiences that exemplify them. Or invite the children to make up fictional situations – playing the 'What if' game often prompts ideas. So for example –

- What if you woke up tomorrow with the body of an animal? (You can choose which animal. You can think like yourself but are unable to speak.) Themes: empathy, compassion, exploitation, the nature of thought.

- What if any harm you directed at another person was reflected back on yourself? (So if you pushed someone hard you would fall down.) Themes: choice, retribution, justice.

- What if when your body died your mind was able to 'jump' into someone else's body? (Think about this in two ways. Firstly, when you jumped in you pushed the other person's mind out. Secondly, when you jumped in the other person's mind stayed but you were in charge of it.) Themes: individuality and identity, the nature of thought

What-ifs can easily be tailored to the age and capabilities of the children you're working with. The ones above are fairly sophisticated and I've used them with Year 6 upwards. Helping children to recognise themes allows them to 'write what they know' at a deeper level even if the story is science fiction, fantasy etc.

Building in a thematic basis to a story or poem can also give the work greater significance and power. In one Year 6 class I visited I met Gabe whose passion was vampires. His teacher bemoaned the fact that the only way to get him to write stories was to let him put vampires in them. In chatting with Gabe we looked at the idea that in some stories the vampire was lonely, felt trapped and isolated from the sweep of human life. We also talked about whether being able to live forever potentially, but only by harming other people, was right. Gabe went on to write 'The lonely vampire', which struck me as being far more poignant than some of his other recent pieces.

4. The building blocks of story

The metaphor of 'building blocks' gives children a concrete image (excuse the pun) to help them understand the levels of construction of a narrative. The themes are like the foundations of a building – but the foundations can support not just one house but a whole row of them. In other words themes that run through one's own life can inform and support any number of pieces of writing.

The 'load bearing walls' or girderwork of the building represent basic narrative elements such as a central problem, the hero, the villain, the hero's journey etc. We might then imagine the separate rooms as being the various genres and forms the writing takes, while the furniture and décor of each room represent individual pieces of work.

- I make a distinction between genre and form. In my mind horror, romance, thriller etc are different genres whereas narrative prose, poetry, essay, letter and so on are distinct written forms. One reason for separating them in this way is explained in the next chapter. I know that some people lump genre and form together under the definition 'kinds of writing'.

7
Themes, genre and forms

Key concept

A core element of creative thinking is about making fresh connections. Linking themes with different genres and written in a variety of forms not only gives children insight into these aspects of literature but helps them to generate new ideas.

Learning benefits

- **Helps children to understand the deep structure of writing.**
- **Offers a novel way to learn about genre and written forms.**
- **Offers a flexible and fruitful technique for generating ideas.**

Activities

1. Genre and form

Use a short story that the children are already familiar with, or run the linking game on page 8 to generate a few 'seed ideas'. Then refer to the grid on page 76 and select a genre and a written form. Or you can roll dice to choose these randomly. Because of the number of categories of genre and form, roll two dice at once for a number between 2 and 12, going 'along the corridor and up the stairs'. So two double rolls give me 7 and 4 – a spy thriller written as a radio play. Another go gives me 6 and 8 – a wild west story written as a newspaper article.

2. Choosing a theme

You can make the activity more challenging by writing theme words on to scraps of paper which, again, can either be chosen deliberately or drawn at random out of an envelope. So as I play this game sitting here at my desk I draw out 'loneliness' and 'independence'. I might choose one of these themes for each of my writing tasks or try and incorporate both into one piece of work.

Some themes are obviously more abstract than others, 'loneliness' for example is probably more directly accessible and understandable to younger children than is 'independence' (remember Gabe's 'The lonely vampire' story mentioned on page 73). Create your collection of theme words with this in mind – typing 'themes' into a search engine will generate plenty of examples, some that are central to a text that you may already be studying with your class.

Genre / Form	Story	Poem	Letter	Diary	News-paper Article	Radio Play	Film Script	Advert	Text Message	Play	Comic Stip
12 Romance											
11 Science Fiction											
10 Fantasy											
9 Horror											
8 Wild West											
7 Murder Mystery											
6 Historical											
5 Pirate											
4 Spy Thriller											
3 Animal Characters											
2 Comedy Adventure											
	2	3	4	5	6	7	8	9	10	11	12

first dice roll

second dice roll

3. Themes in non-fiction

As children become familiar with the idea of themes in fiction they will be more readily able to recognise and explore them in non-fictional contexts. News reporting (including the letters' pages and editorial comment) and advertising are two obvious arenas for 'theme spotting'.

Just glancing through a few pages of a weekly magazine brings up the following advertisements –

- Holidays in Cyprus – escape, cuisine from around the world/international flavours, desire for something more.
- Smart TV – connectivity, performance, cutting edge.
- Health supplements – living longer (fear of death?), youthfulness.

Most advertisements offer rich pickings when you want children to practise 'being nosy' through noticing and questioning. The thematic underpinning of ads is brought out in both their visuals and the linguistic techniques used, including use of strong verbs and adjectives, superlatives, comparatives, alliteration and rhyme (often found in catch phrases). Looking for these will also throw up plenty of emotive words and persuasive tricks. For older students a particularly useful source of things to look for can be found at http://home.olemiss.edu/~egjbp/comp/ad-claims.html.

Ask children to create slogans for products that already exist or ones they invent. These adjectives and verbs are the ones that most commonly appear in marketing blurb and advertisements – new, good, better, best, free, fresh, delicious, full, sure, clean, wonderful, special, crisp, fine, big, great, real, easy, bright, extra, safe, rich, make, get, give, have, see, buy, come, go, know, keep, look, need, love, use, feel, like, choose, take, start, taste. (The word 'slogan derives from the Gaelic sluagh-ghairm meaning 'battle cry'!)

For example –

CrispyCrunch Bar – The big bite that's 'choc' full of goodness.

Zippyzap Furniture Polish – Brings out the richness of wood, keeps your furniture looking good.

Freshenup Washing Powder – Give your clothes that special softness.

4. Themes in philosophy

Developing philosophy for children (P4C) in school has been mentioned elsewhere in the book and complements the kinds of thinking we want them to do as they become better writers. Philosophy is a way of exploring fundamental problems connected for instance with existence and the nature of reality, mind and consciousness, knowledge and meaning, morality and values.

Raising awareness of the themes of philosophical enquiry with children is often done using stories as a stimulus. In 'Little Red Riding Hood' for example we find the concepts of family, punishment, revenge, deception, innocence, nature versus culture, obedience. Whereas in a P4C session these would be used to generate 'juicy' questions for enquiry, they can also form the basis of further stories, poems etc that children can write for themselves.

- Pick a fairy tale or nursery rhyme and brainstorm its underpinning concepts with the class. Take one or two of these and play the what-if game (page 73) to create different scenarios that form the basis of other versions of the story.

Teacher tip

If you run this activity regularly you'll soon have built up a resource bank of both meaty concepts and plot ideas.

- Mini-moral dilemmas. These can be used as the basis for discussion prior to writing. Here are some that have worked well.

It is the world of the future. The only way you can prevent your family from starving is by stealing food. Would you do it? Would you steal food from a big supermarket? Would you steal food from your neighbour up the road? Would you do it if you knew that the other person's family would starve if you took the food? What other ways can you see to solve the problem?

You see your friend cheating in a written test. You know that if anyone is caught cheating the whole class will be punished and shamed. But you also know that your friend is likely to fail the test if he or she doesn't cheat. Would you tell on your friend? What would you do if, knowing you were likely to fail the test too, your friend offered to share answers? What if your friend's mum was very ill in hospital and quite likely to die?

It is the future (again)! The human population of Earth has increased so much that we are in danger of extinction due to huge wars over water and food. The world government suggests that if everyone over

30 agreed to be killed painlessly, the human race would survive and life would quickly become better for everyone. Do you agree with the World Government's plan in principle? Would you agree with it if the age limit were different? Whatever the age limit, would you make any exceptions to the rule? Why?

(These themes have been brilliantly explored in the classic science fiction novels *Make Room, Make Room!* by Harry Harrison (filmed as Soylent Green) and *Logan's Run* by William F. Nolan (film of the same name). These are novels and films suitable for Key Stage 3 and older.)

A wizard offers you a potion that will keep you healthy and young looking for the next 100 years. However, people around you will age more quickly and their health will grow worse. In other words, they will be paying the price for your good fortune. What do you say to the wizard (clean language only please)? What if the people who were to suffer were complete strangers to you? What if the people who were to suffer had all committed bad crimes? What if the sufferers were not people but animals?

The reader's focus of attention

> **Key concept**
>
> Generally speaking a writer will know more about a story than she puts into it. Selecting which details to include and directing the mind's eye of the reader are important skills to develop.

Learning benefits

- **Emphasises the principle that 'nothing is ever wasted'. Even details that are not included in a piece of work help to inform what the writer does put in (and can in any case often be used elsewhere).**
- **Highlights the importance that everything a writer does include is there for a good reason. This helps to eliminate the tendency to grab at the first thought that springs to mind.**
- **Leads to recognition that language is influential, and that choosing how ideas are framed in writing creates a more memorable experience for the reader.**

For the first few activities we'll use the opening of a short story called *Roboville*.

Roboville

'Tina Taylor put down her book and smiled as the lawn mower trundled out of the garage. She checked the time on her mobile. It was ten o'clock on this Saturday morning. At least the robot-mower's task program was working properly. Tina's father Professor Tom Taylor had been having a little trouble lately getting his inventions to do what he wanted them to, *when* he wanted them to do it. Perhaps he'd sorted out that problem now. Fingers crossed, thought Tina.

'She watched the smart silver machine glide along the edge of the front lawn quietly and efficiently. A green light at the front blinked on and off – all systems AOK. At the back of the mower a large bag collected the cuttings . . . But the bag seemed to be growing very large very quickly. Surely it couldn't be gathering that much grass and leaves?

'Suddenly there came a clanking noise from the utility room nearby, then a dull *boom* and a gurgling sound. A strange creature made of soap bubbles stumbled out into the garden, coughing and spluttering.

' Tim?' Tina wondered. She was frightened and worried for a second, then laughed as her twin brother wiped the suds off his face and glared at her.'

Now instruct the children to try the following:

1. Reading with attention

Notice what you're imagining. As your eyes scan the words your imagination creates sights, maybe sounds, feelings and other information. Make notes about what you saw, heard etc. Use the following questions to help you.

- What is the weather like?
- How old do you imagine Tim and Tina to be?
- What kind of house do they live in?
- What do you notice about the street where the Taylors live?
- What does the robot lawn mower look like?

2. Adding details

Your imagination works fast and enjoys making pictures and sounds. Create a few more details in your imagined scene. Write each detail on a scrap of paper and put them in an envelope. Work with a few friends so that you have plenty of scraps to choose from. Pick them out one at a time and notice how your imagination uses them. Here are a few ideas to start you off –

- There is a wooden trellis on the wall to the right of the front door. A tall rose bush in bloom is climbing up it.
- Tom Taylor is tinkering with a new invention in the garage.
- An ice-cream van drives slowly down the street, its chimes playing. It stops nearby and a few children come running to buy ices.

Teacher tip

Sometimes a detail will not fit with a child's imagined scenario, in which case he or she can discard it.

---

3. Noticing clues

When you imagined the scene of Tina in the garden you probably created a rich picture effortlessly. Imagine a blue inflatable paddling pool on the lawn – see, you did it straight away and it was easy. Now imagine a T rex loping down the middle of the road. The children run away screaming. The ice-cream man scrambles out of his van just in time as the T-Rex stamps on it with a huge hind limb, crumpling it like a cardboard box.

Even though the T rex situation could never happen (as far as we know!), you probably imagined it just as clearly as you did the paddling pool. Our imaginations working in this way are not critical. That is, you don't mentally say to yourself 'I'm not going to imagine that T rex in the street. It's impossible, they're extinct!' This is why we can read and write about impossible things – and imagine things that may one day be possible.

However, you can read with a more critical, logical eye. See if you can work out why these statements may be true by looking for clues in the opening of Roboville.

a. Tim and Tina are the same age.

b. Tom Taylor is a very educated man.

c. The Taylors live in a large house.

d. The house is not one of a terrace.

e. The weather is fine.

f. It is late summer/early autumn.

Answers

a. They are twins.

b. He is a professor. The fact that he invents things also suggests he is clever.

c. The house has a utility room and garage nearby. Small houses are not as likely to have a utility room, and either there will be no garage or it will be one of a block some distance away.

d. Same reasons as iii. Also, while terraced houses might have small front gardens they probably don't have front lawns big enough to need a lawn mower.

e. Tina watches the lawn mower appear from the garage on to the front lawn. She would be most likely to see this if she was outside. If she's outside reading a book the weather must be fine. Also, lawns are best mown when the grass is dry.

f. The lawn mower picks up leaves as well as grass. This suggests leaves have started to fall from nearby bushes and trees, which is most likely to be in late summer or early autumn. If it were later in the autumn the weather is less likely to be warm enough for Tina to sit outside reading.

Practice in reading with a more critical eye helps to develop children's editorial skills. Look at page 104 to see how Bita improved her work by spotting logical errors in the first draft. An enjoyable variation of the activity is to spot logical and continuity errors in films. Two useful websites are www.slipups.com and www.moviemistakes.com, or visit YouTube. Obviously, check that the clips you intend to show the class are appropriately rated.

4. **Point of view**

● The scene is written from Tina's point of view but in the third person. Rewrite it (or part of it) in the first person.

- Imagine what's happening to Tim in the utility room and write the story opening from his point of view.

5. Tone

The author has tried to create a light, humorous tone for the story. What images help to achieve this? What changes would you make if you wanted the opening of the story to be 'darker' and more dramatic?

Teacher tip

Changes of vocabulary to characters' reactions are obvious targets. Here's the first paragraph rewritten with (hopefully) the darker tone we're looking for.

'Tina Taylor frowned on hearing the sound; a grinding rattle that grated on her nerves. She put down her book and glanced worriedly towards her father's garage-laboratory. A moment later the automated lawn mower came trundling out on to the lawn. She checked the time on her mobile. It was ten o'clock on this Saturday morning. Perhaps this time the robot-mower's task program would work properly. Professor Taylor had been having technical difficulties lately with several of his inventions and there had been a couple of mishaps that Tina didn't care to think about. Perhaps he'd sorted out the mower problem now. But even as the thought crossed her mind Tina knew she wasn't convinced. In fact she had a bad feeling about the whole thing.'

---

6. Age and language level

When authors plan a children's story one of the early decisions they make is what age group they are writing for. The main child-characters in such a story are usually the same age as or a bit older than the readership. What age range do you think Roboville is aimed at? What clues do find in a) the language itself and b) the style of humour?

Note: Roboville was written for fairly competent readers aged between seven and nine. Most slightly younger readers could understand the story if it was read to them.

Planning strategies

Key concepts

In encouraging young writers we must strike a balance between getting them to think beyond the first idea and losing interest through 'overthinking' or following prescribed planning strategies too rigidly. While some generic advice will be useful for everyone, children are likely to develop (with your guidance) their own working methods, especially if this is encouraged within the classroom environment and the creative ethos mentioned in previous chapters.

Learning benefits

- **Offers a 'menu' of planning strategies and encourages children to discover which is/are most appropriate to their learning style and preferred way of working.**
- **Reinforces the notion that achieving 'high standards' does not always mean the same thing as being told 'the right way to do it'.**
- **Encourages the creative ethos of adapting techniques so that they become more effective at an individual level.**
- **Encourages the sharing of good ideas and practice.**

All written forms have a deliberate structure which has evolved over time (and is still evolving) into what can conveniently be called the conventions of form. In other words the layout of a piece of writing will incorporate features that we would conventionally expect to find there. So as we all know a story has a beginning, a middle and an end which constitute one of the most basic conventions of that and just about every other form of writing. Refinements to that fundamental structure in narrative include: flashbacks (to help establish 'back story'); subplots; foreshadowing (where a feature that becomes important later is mentioned early on); story 'arcs' (an extended storyline running across a series of episodic adventures); sequels; prequels and so on. Note that these conventions and refinements do not confine themselves to entirely text-based stories: they also appear in film; TV; theatre productions; comic books and video games.

It's often the case however that many innovative writers, filmmakers etc will bend the rules (again deliberately) to create unconventional work in order to explore their themes. (Remember Basho's advice to 'learn the rules well and then you can bend them' – page 16.) While unconventionality for its own sake has little merit in my opinion, its use as a purposive and creative force breaks new ground and drives the evolution of the art form.

Activities

1. The vocabulary of the form

Familiarise children with the relevant vocabulary of a range of written forms. So in the case of stories, the items mentioned above – story arc, prequel and others. Alternatively newspapers come as tabloids and (less commonly now) broadsheets and feature boxes, bylines, captions and columns, fillers, kickers, logos, news holes, reefers and many more. (I admit I didn't know about some of these until I researched this section.

Teacher tip

You might find it appropriate to ask the children themselves to do some research. In the case of the vocabulary of newspapers, magazines and films especially their findings can be incorporated into rich and colourful displays.

---

2. The etymology of writing

Looking at the origins of some of the terms used in various written forms not only provides useful insights but often gives children concrete metaphors that they can visualise more easily (such as the fact that 'text' shares its root with 'textiles' and means 'to weave'). Once children appreciate this you can extend the metaphor to talk about patterns within a story, the fabric of a story, richly woven ideas, embellishing a narrative and, as an experiment, ask the class to discuss what 'Cutting your coat according to your cloth' might mean in the context of their writing. Here are a few interesting word roots to start you off:

- Legend from Latin 'to gather, select, read'. Akin to the Greek legein meaning 'to gather, say'. Interestingly the root is shared by the word lesson, which originally meant 'the act of reading'.
- Lyric from the Greek relating to 'singing to the lyre', hence the origin of lyric poetry.
- Narrate from Latin meaning 'to know', 'to be acquainted with'.
- Poem from the Greek meaning 'to make or compose'.
- Story from the Latin 'historia', from Greek meaning 'inquiry', which traces back to 'knowing', 'learned'.
- Tale from Old Norse talu, 'talk' and possibly back to the Latin dolus, 'guile', 'deceit'.
- Tell from Old High German 'to count' (hence a bank teller) but also with links to talu, 'tale'.
- Word from the Latin verbum and back to the Greek eirein, 'to say, speak'.

Teacher tip

Once you have accumulated some origins challenge the children with questions about how the original meanings of the words differ from or relate to their modern usage. For example –

- Can you think of any connections between the words 'legend' and 'lesson' as we use them now?
- How can the word 'narrative' be applied to something other than a short story or a novel?
- How can we learn or come to know things from stories if they are supposed to be made up and not true (see page 61)?
- The word tale was perhaps originally linked with the idea of trickery or trying to deceive. Do you think that any trace of that old meaning still exists in the way we use that word today?

Take it further

Much of the vocabulary of language is taken for granted. We use terms like adjective, comma, noun, phrase, punctuation, sentence and many more. While our aim is to teach children what these words refer to, I suspect that little time is devoted to where the terms came from. Again, dipping into the past can draw out some fascinating insights:

- Adjective comes from Latin meaning 'attached or added'.

- Comma means 'piece which is cut off', in the sense that the comma separates or cuts off phrases and clauses in a sentence.
- Noun comes from Latin nomon meaning 'name'.
- Phrase comes from Greek 'to point out, express, tell', going back further to phrazesthai 'to consider', of unknown origin (according to http://etymonline.com/).
- Punctuation comes from Latin 'marking with points or dots'.
- Sentence comes from L. sententia, 'thought, meaning, judgment, opinion'. The definition of a sentence as a grammatically complete statement supposedly dates from the mid-fifteenth century out of the idea that a sentence is 'meaningful', i.e. makes sense within itself.

1. Visual planning

Visual planners allow all of the ideas that a child has created to be available at a glance. This increases the probability of fresh connections being made and breaks the tendency to think only in a beginning-middle-end sequence. We've already looked at the basic narrative line (page 48) and the more sophisticated 'lazy eight' narrative template (page 59), while the 'story hill' is used commonly in schools. Here are some further ideas.

The story hill is useful for structuring a narrative in terms of introduction, build up, dilemma, resolution, ending. Once children are familiar with this basic pattern use the story hill more flexibly. So for instance a template like Figure 21 encourages children to change pace, build tension and create peaks of excitement and drama. Different 'hilly patterns' focus children's thinking in this way on a scene-by-scene basis and offer a range (as it were) of options for structuring stories.

Teacher tip

Give each child or group a large sheet of paper on which to draw their hills so that there's plenty of room to attach sticky notes as they plan. The question star coin flip game (page 48) can be used where required to flesh out further details.

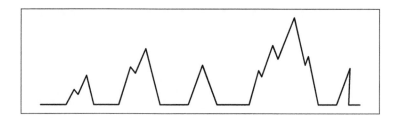

You can use the same technique to familiarise children with basic narrative elements such as hero, villain, partner etc and also to guide their planning without overly spoon-feeding them with ideas, as shown here.

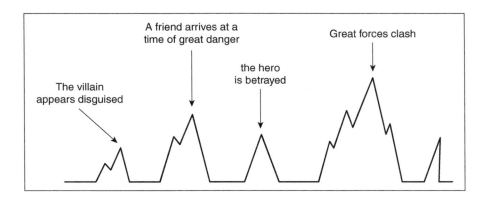

The villain appears disguised

A friend arrives at a time of great danger

the hero is betrayed

Great forces clash

2. Map maker

Again using large sheets of paper, ask children to draw the kind of landscape where they want the action to take place (they can draw several maps if the story happens in various locations). A picture can be used as a stimulus. So as an example the desert scene on page 22 might lead to a map where a range of mesas crosses from west to east, there's a canyon to the north and hills nearby in the south. Mark the cardinal compass points and number them 1–4. This allows dice rolls to be incorporated into the game if required. Four-sided dice can be obtained from online stores and specialist toyshops, or use standard six-sided dice and discard 5 and 6 when they appear.

Six-sided dice can be used in another way however. Ask the class to come up with sets of six options under a range of headings such as 'something is found', 'an unexpected crisis', 'a new character appears' etc. Each list is given a different colour that matches the colours of the dice you're using. Whenever a child is stuck for an idea, she decides what category she wants to pick from and rolls the corresponding colour dice to select an option at random. Often, 'taking your mind by surprise' in this way sparks off a fresh idea. Occasionally when the option is chosen a child will say 'Oh but I wanted such-and-such to happen'. In this case the child knows her own mind, so allow her to discard the chosen option in favour of the one she prefers.

It's likely that the class will come up with more than six options for the different categories. In this case, get the children to write them out on sets of coloured cards. These are shuffled and placed face-down on a table. Whenever a child needs a 'creative boost' she goes to the table to select a chance card under her chosen category.

Coin flips are useful for generating ideas in this activity too. So let's suppose coin and dice are being used. The technique works as follows. Begin the story (or scene) by prompting a decision. For example 'Six bandits suddenly appear out of the hills. They are approaching you fast. What could you do?' Ask for an either-or: either stand your ground and fight (heads) or turn and run (tails). Flip the coin. Let's say it's tails. 'You turn and run, but which way? Pick two directions that would increase your chances of escape'. So either east (heads) or west (tails) where you might lose the bandits. Flip the coin. Heads. 'You go east but suddenly encounter a problem. Give me an either-or…'

Again, children can usually think of more than two options. However listening to them all will slow up the game, so I think it works best if the children get into the action quickly and think at a fast pace so that the story remains more interesting for them.

So the game proceeds. The coins/dice are there to kickstart the story or scene and also help if a child gets stuck. At any point they can be abandoned if a child knows her own mind or wants to make a decision (for a reason she has considered).

Because this is just the planning stage children only need to make brief notes on the map. Use of the narrative line, the lazy-eight template or story-hill variants can be used subsequently to flesh out the plot.

3. If-then trees

Children work in pairs or threes for this. Use a large sheet of paper and write an exciting kickstarter sentence at the bottom, having chosen a genre and setting. So 'Bandits attack'. Ask for two possible options (if you've already played the map maker game you can recycle ideas from there). Let's say you're given 'Fight' and 'Run'. Consider each one in turn and ask for two options each time. So 'If we fight then?' (get killed/get captured). 'If we run then?' (escape/get captured). Pick one of these and run the process through again. 'If we get captured then?' (ransomed/pumped for information)... You can carry on creating branches until a workable storyline emerges or there are no more options. Children can then go back to any other branch that has not been explored and 'grow' it further. A complex branching tree of possible storylines quickly appears. Children can then follow one or 'cherry pick' ideas from different branches to construct a new narrative.

Making if-then trees has a number of benefits-

- Young writers are encouraged to think of two ideas each time and consider the consequences of any given option.

- Asking children to justify the options they choose helps to develop their reasoning abilities.

- The activity promotes discussion and collaborative construction of narrative.

- Children come to realise that making a story is not a matter of struggling to find enough ideas, but of using judgement and discrimination in cutting out less interesting or viable options in favour of the most exciting, dramatic, etc storyline.

- More implicitly, young writers gain an appreciation of the 'principle of potential'; the notion that from the simplest of starting points a rich harvest of ideas can be gathered (or as one ten-year-old said to me 'I never realised it before, but stories are everywhere!').

4. Board games

The most obvious benefits for children in creating board games are that they provide a context for instructional writing, aid inventiveness and sharpen reasoning skills as rules, rewards and forfeits are discussed. Combining the creation of board games with story making boosts the learning value of the activity. Two examples appear below but many other versions of the basic idea are possible. A third example appears on page 87 as a further use for the 'story grid'.

Story Map

- Use a simple drawn map such as the one opposite. This might be one that the children have already created from the map maker activity on page 85, in which case the genre and some notion of the storyline will already have been determined. If the map is being constructed from scratch ask the children to decide on the genre first, which will guide them in choosing a setting. Once the drawing has been done add a numbered route and then groups can set about deciding on the rules and instructions.

The game can also feature to a greater or lesser degree the structure of the basic narrative template we looked at on page 59. Note that the numbered route itself doesn't have to be in the lazy-eight shape (though it can be), but rather that some or all of the significant narrative points can appear along the way. So for example –

- Call to action. Sheriff Jim James hears news that a gang of bandits is terrorising settlers to the south-east. Look at the list of provisions and decide which three items are likely to be most useful on your journey. Each item carries a certain number of points. Once you've chosen check with the Games Master (teacher or group that made the game) how many points your selection has earned. Then roll the dice to move on.

- Threshold guardian. You meet a tribal elder and ask him the best way to cross the desert. He says he will tell you but you must either give him half of your earned points or solve a riddle. Choose now.

- Point of greatest ordeal. You enter the old Clampit Mine and find it to be a maze of tunnels. You have one minute to find your way through the maze. This will bring you to the place where your kidnapped friend has been hidden. For each five seconds you take beyond the minute you must sacrifice one of your earned points. If you fail to escape the maze once your last point has gone you lose the game.

Inventing instructions like these creates the opportunity to introduce or revisit second person writing (you/your). Also note that instructions can be as simple or elaborate as you or the children want them to be. The ones above are fairly complex and require players to reason, make decisions and keep cool under pressure – so thinking skills can be built in as part of the game play.

You can of course choose the context of the activity yourself and relate it to a current topic. So if you were studying the Ancient Egyptians the genre, map and vocabulary list would all be linked to that subject.

Dodgem

- For this you will need a game board such as the one below. I've used a 12 x 12 grid and nine target (starred) squares for each player. A grid of around 144 squares makes for a game of reasonable length and pitches the tension of play just right. You can increase or decrease the number of target squares as you wish. You will also need a four-sided dice (or a six-sided where rolls of five or six are discarded), a different coloured counter for each team and enough counters of a third colour to eventually cover all of the starred squares.

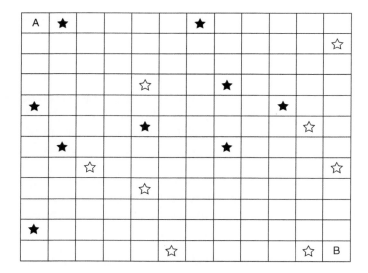

- The game is for two players or small teams. Each team is represented by a different colour counter. Flip a coin to determine which player/team goes first, then roll the dice to see how many squares that player may move. Movement can be in any direction. A-player must visit all of the white stars and answer a question each time. B-player must visit all of the black stars and answer a question each time. If a question is answered correctly the player may move a further square in any direction, either to get closer to the next star or further away from the opponent. Each time a question is correctly answered that player gains a point (noted on a tally card) and a counter of the third colour is placed on that square to show it has been visited. If a question is answered incorrectly the player must stay on the starred square until his next turn.

- Players can also 'hunt' each other by trying to land on the same square as the opponent. Suppose after rolling the dice B-player is within range of A-player, he can move to A-player's square and occupy it at the same time. A-player then has the option of giving up a certain number of points (decided beforehand or determined now with a dice roll), or answering a question. If the question is answered correctly A-player keeps his points and has a double dice roll (to get away from the enemy!). If the question is answered wrongly A-player must forfeit double points. The winner of the game is the player who has most points once the last starred square on the board has been visited.

- If you want the children to make their own game board be sure that they position the stars fairly so that neither player is disadvantaged. Questions can be on any topic (again, perhaps a topic you are currently studying, a book you are reading with the class etc) and pitched according to the age and ability level of the players – however one variation is to make the questions harder the further a player gets from his home square.

Story grid

- This activity uses a 6 x 6 grid of pictures (or words and pictures) such as the one below. Any grid is genre based and so should feature genre-specific images as well as some generalised visuals and a few that are deliberately vague or ambiguous. Each child or working group will also need a six-sided dice.

- Images are selected by dice rolls. Use the co-ordinates rule of 'along the corridor and up the stairs'. Be sure that children count their first number beneath the bottom row of the grid. Thus, 3/3 brings you to the maze, 5/2 to the guards etc.

- Roll the dice to choose two images to begin with and (as in the linking game on page 8) ask 'If these were used in a story, what would the story be about?' Or you can say 'As soon as we land on the second picture we can put the two images together and they will tell us something about the story.'

- The emphasis of this second question is subtly different from the first. Suggesting the two images will tell us about the story and builds a presupposition of success into what you say (this is more likely to be subconsciously registered than consciously noticed). The phrase 'something about' is 'artfully vague', which is to say that the outcome of the children's thinking is certain – we will gain ideas about the story – but what these are and how each child creates depends upon each individual. The second question also more elegantly accommodates the fact that some children will have a large scale overview idea as they make a connection, while others will generate small scale details. So a roll of 4/1 big tree and 5/4 blade might produce 'The king of the land decides to cut down all of the trees in his kingdom' or 'A traveller finds a sword among the roots of a tree'.

- If you demonstrate the story grid activity with the whole class each picture selection will produce a number of ideas. It isn't usually possible to accommodate them all: ideas might be contradictory and will in any case quickly lead to a very confusing plot! So it's best to explain at the outset that you will pick only one child's idea each time. Those that are not used can be written down on scraps of paper and put into a treasure box of ideas for future use. The treasure box tactic explicitly values the thinking of every child who contributes and quickly builds into a useful classroom resource. Subsequently, individuals or groups can sift through the treasure box of ideas to generate new plotlines. The box also reinforces the notion that in becoming better writers nothing is ever wasted.

- Let's suppose we select: The king of the land decides to cut down all of the trees in his kingdom. You or the children must now come up with a question that will allow you to learn more about the story. The obvious question is why does the king want to chop down all his trees? Roll the dice twice to select a further image that will answer the question or at least give you a clue. So 6/1 – carved wooden house. Some of the drawings in this grid are based on actual wooden sculptures created by Peter Leadbeater (www.peterleadbeater.com) and form a story trail at East Carlton Park in Northamptonshire.

- My idea was that the king wanted the wood to create many sculpted houses for the people of his kingdom. There are many other possibilities of course so, time permitting, here is an opportunity to discuss the ideas to see how well they work; how reasonable and convincing they are, how well they fit in with other ideas the class comes up with.

Teacher tip

Emphasise to the children that it's fine to test out an idea rigorously in terms of believability, logical consistency and so on, but that no criticism is ever implied of the child who thought of it.

- If we go with the idea of the king wanting to provide houses for his subjects, a number of follow-on questions are possible, such as: Why wooden houses? Why do they need to be carved? How come so many people in the kingdom suddenly need homes? The game proceeds by 'following the question trail', taking one or more of the questions generated by the previous dice roll. Usually children need only play the game for ten or 15 minutes before they have a plot roughed out. Ideas can be organised using the narrative line (page 48) or narrative template (page 59) techniques discussed earlier.

Further notes

- Some children soon abandon the random factor of dice rolls. They know how their story will turn out and want to choose images for themselves. I always allow this.
- If a child becomes confused by too much information, ask him/her to tell you what bit(s) of the story she's already clear about. Then delete the confusing stuff. Ask the child to roll the dice to choose a picture that will tell him something that happens right at the very end of the story. Psychologically she has now bypassed the vague or confusing middle and will usually come up with an idea that links the story's ending and early stages. The middle now in most cases becomes clear.
- Make sure that each child or group asks a question before rolling the dice again. Some children simply roll dice and make a list of the pictures they've landed on. These have not been connected up and the children have no idea what their story will be about.
- You can find much more information on the story grid technique (plus a selection of over a dozen grids) in *Developing Literacy and Creative Writing Through Storymaking* – see Bibliography.

Take it further

- Although the story grid game as it stands works over a wide age and ability range, you can make it more sophisticated by incorporating a 'concept' or 'theme' grid into the activity. As well as rolling dice to select images on the story grid itself, roll to select one or more concepts/themes from the secondary grid. This can be done at the start of the activity and also as the story evolves in answer to questions about a character's personality or motivation, the reasons behind an event and so on. Some suggested themes are: superstition, thoughtfulness, wisdom, famine, growth, partnership, breaking, companionship, trust, honour, resistance, balance, communication, foolishness, triumph, reversal, loyalty, disruption, loss, movement, prophecy, betrayal, trickery, responsibility, faith, illusion, enchantment, impulsiveness, theft, healing, possessiveness, defence, celebration, retreat, protection, help.
- Children can create their own story grids based on favourite books, movies, comics etc. This allows them to use characters and settings that they are already familiar with and yet come up with fresh ideas.
- Story grids can also be built around topic areas from other subjects. Groups I've worked with have made grids on the Anglo Saxons, Ancient Egyptians, the Romans, landscapes and wildlife of Africa, the Apollo missions to the Moon, Ice Age Britain and many others.

Teacher tip

Supply items of vocabulary from the topic that the children can build in to their stories.

- Number the boxes of the story grid in a zigzag fashion starting from the bottom left-hand corner (as in Snakes and Ladders). Split the class into four groups. Each group must come up with 36 questions, one that is either relevant in some way to each of the pictures or to the genre/topic in general (and that has a chance of being answered by the other groups!). Number the groups 1–4, give each a different coloured counter and then roll a four-sided dice to determine which group goes first. Let's say it's Group 3. One child from Group 3 rolls a six-sided dice to land on one of the squares along the bottom row. Roll the four-sided dice to determine which other group asks Group 3 the question they thought of relevant to that square (obviously if a three comes up roll again). If Group 3 answers correctly they gain a point. If they answer wrongly the team asking the question gains a point.

The game proceeds as above. Once the starting order of the groups has been established it remains that way for the rest of the game. The winning group is not the one to reach the end first (i.e. square 36 in the top left-hand corner), but the team that has accumulated the most points.

1. Plot templates

These are blocked-out areas on a page that guide young writers through the basic structure of a story, such that they end up with a 'route map' of the narrative. Minimal notes are made at this stage, which means that children don't feel they are 'writing it all out again' when they tackle the first draft. Plot templates are quick and easy to create and can be based on existing stories. The example over the page gives a flavour of the idea.

2. Seed thoughts

I've mentioned elsewhere that much of the thinking going on prior to writing happens subconsciously. The outcomes of this 'behind the scenes' processing spring into consciousness as sudden insights (Aha! moments), fresh connections, new directions and a growing sense that the story will work. Subconscious involvement also manifests itself in the language 'flowing' as the writing occurs; the almost effortless outpouring of sentences that often takes the writer by surprise. Most experienced writers I'm sure will admit to being quietly impressed with themselves from time to time as a beautifully crafted sentence or paragraph, or a startlingly vivid image, appears out of the blue coupled perhaps with the thought 'Wow, I didn't know I could do that!'. The writer Douglas Hill told me that his last book 'Felt as though it was being dictated to me by my main character. I just sat there and wrote down what he had to say.'

Although cultivating this 'working partnership' between the conscious and subconscious realms of the mind takes time, subconscious processing can be stimulated by a simple yet elegant technique known as seed thoughts. The idea is simply to plant the seed of a story in the mind and forget about it for awhile, though making sure you have some way of reminding yourself about it later. The seed might be a simple connection such as those generated by the linking game on page 8. Or you might tell yourself that 'by tomorrow afternoon I'll have learned much more about my main character.' Or 'by Friday I'll know how my story will end.' Consciously framing these intentions 'primes' the subconscious to carry out the task. Since the subconscious mind is the repository of our memories and experiences it is a fantastic resource when it comes to creating new information.

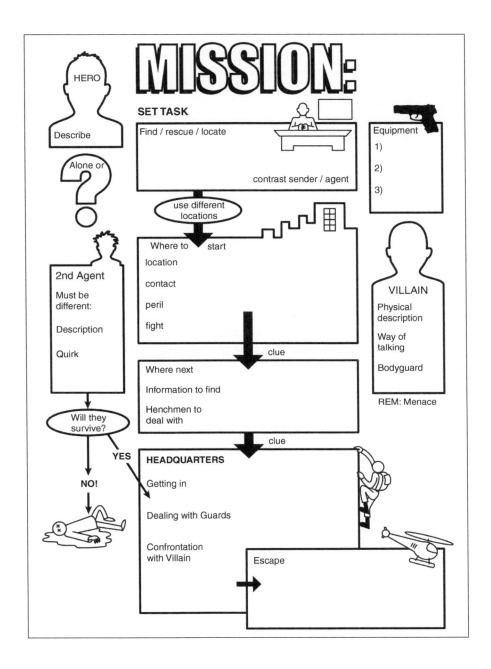

MISSION:

SET TASK

Find / rescue / locate

contrast sender / agent

HERO

Describe

Alone or **?**

Equipment
1)
2)
3)

2nd Agent

Must be different:

Description

Quirk

use different locations

Where to start

location

contact

peril

fight

clue

Where next

Information to find

Henchmen to deal with

clue

VILLAIN

Physical description

Way of talking

Bodyguard

REM: Menace

Will they survive?

YES

NO!

HEADQUARTERS

Getting in

Dealing with Guards

Confrontation with Villain

Escape

Another aspect of subconscious activity is the 'filter effect'. Suppose I want to learn more about a character in a story I'm planning. I tell myself that's what will happen and then let go of it (the seed has been planted so why bother fiddling with the soil?). Almost uncannily then I find myself noticing people, snippets of conversation, objects, events etc that fit perfectly with my intention to develop the character in question.

Practically speaking, you can stimulate subconscious processing in the children in any number of ways:

- If you want the children to write a story on Monday, tell them about it on Friday. 'On Monday we'll be planning a story about a secret agent who breaks into the villain's headquarters to stop him taking over the world!' Then leave it. Through the weekend the children will be subconsciously gathering up ideas that fit the task in hand. On Monday allow ten minutes' quiet writing time for them to jot down anything about the story that comes to mind. Many will be surprised that they know more than they thought they did.

Teacher tip

The technique works for fact-based topics too. If you're starting on the Victorians next week, tell the class about that now.

- Notes to self. If a child is having problems with a piece of creative work, suggest that she writes a note to herself, stating the problem together with the clear intention that she'll solve it soon. Keep the note safe and give it back after the agreed time. She may well have found the solution already, but if not might well have a clear insight now.
- Future diary. The technique here is to get the child to pretend that she can hop into the future and become an older, wiser, more experienced writer in order to solve a writing problem. Suggest the idea the day before you ask her to write the future diary. Then, next day, give her some quiet time for future-self to write the entry containing the advice she is looking for.

While the seed thought technique is not infallible, it becomes more and more reliable with practice. The sure sign of subconscious activity – the 'flow' I've mentioned – is its effortlessness. There is no struggle as the words appear, nor is there the need to work things out 'logically'. The writing appears as it were, organically, rather than through any mechanical sequential process.

3. Templates for other written forms
   - Magazine article. The inverted pyramid template below is a useful visual to help children understand the importance of grabbing the reader's attention straight away and structuring the piece so that it 'comes to the point' with the conclusion.

     The hook – This part of the article should reel the reader in and capture their attention at once. You need a strong or interesting point in the hook that will encourage the reader to keep reading.

     The summary – The summary should basically sum up what the article is about. Give the supporting points and facts later. The reader should be able to see in a clear and concise format what the rest of the article will contain.

     The body – This is where you include all the support points in a logical and understandable way. Include strong points that help support your focus of the article. Don't just throw in information to take up space or add to the word count. Make sure the points you are using help the focus of the entire article. Weaker points should be combined with strong points to further make your point or just thrown out altogether if they do not contribute to the article as a whole. You also need to make sure your points are interesting and not just a listing of facts which the reader will find boring.

The conclusion – This draws the main threads of the article together and ends with your viewpoint and/or a strong final statement that will linger in the reader's mind.

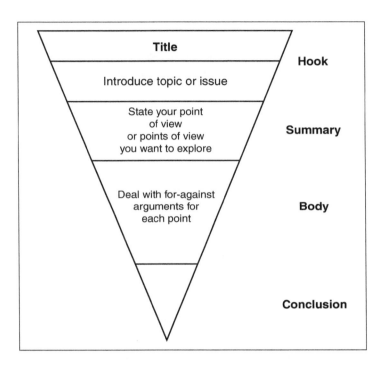

4. Newspaper report

A right-way-up pyramid makes a useful template when you want children to construct a news report. Divide the pyramid shape into five sections: if you do this on an A3 sheet the limited space for writing means that words have to be carefully chosen. The structure of the report comes under the headings of –

Headline – Use only strong 'information carrying' words and leave out packaging such as 'a', 'and', 'the', etc.

Byline – This is an opening sentence that grabs the reader's attention and acts as a bridge between the headline and the body of the report. The byline might be a question, an unusual fact or a startling quote.

First paragraph – This primes the reader to want to know more. It should answer the key open questions of: what, where, when, who and why.

Development of key ideas – Now give the details in a sequence of crisply written paragraphs. Spice up the report by including a few quotes from people you've interviewed. Write in the third person and use the active voice. Be objective – that is, report the facts without distortion.

Last paragraph – This rounds off the report, sometimes in the form of a quote or a catchy sentence that will stick in the reader's memory.

Teacher tip

Some newspaper articles are not objective of course and contain hidden biases and all kinds of linguistic tricks to influence the reader's opinion. Once children become more experienced reporters and can write balanced, unbiased reports you might set them the task of deliberately trying to sway opinion.

---

5. Balanced argument

The 'reason tree' is a useful visual planner that helps children not just to gather the points they want to make but also to assess their robustness. The activity is usually more enjoyable if children work in groups. Supply each group with a large sheet of paper and instruct them to draw the tree shape leaving plenty of room 'under the soil' and to one side.

Once the group has decided on the topic to be argued the children can begin collecting reasons for and against. One set of reasons will become the roots of the tree (let's say 'for' in this case) and the other set gusts of wind represented by arrows coming in from the side. The group must discuss the strength of each reason in turn. Strong reasons for or against can be justified logically through reasoning or be backed up by evidence or facts. Once the robustness of a reason has been agreed it must be written inside either a root or a wind-arrow. The thickness of these reflects the strength of the reasons.

The reason tree (sometimes used as a technique in P4C) also acts as a useful metaphor when explaining how arguments are constructed. Are points rooted in sound thinking? Do the reasons that make up a point of view sway opinion? Does the counterpointing of reasons for and against a proposition help understanding to grow and branch out into new ideas or ways of looking?

Once the planning has been done the children write their arguments according to your preferred structure. A standard model is –

Title – A sentence stating the topic to be discussed. Sometimes the title is in the form of a question.

Introduction – An opening paragraph stating the writer's point of view or the different points of view that will be explored.

Development – Points for and against can either be explored alternately, or the entire argument for can be stated followed by the entire argument against. Sometimes writers put the strongest points/reasons at the end of this section.

Summary and conclusion – A restatement of the writer's opening position or a decision about which view is considered the stronger, and why.

More information on structuring non-fictional forms of writing can be found in *Countdown to Non-Fiction Writing*.

Pen to paper

'Brevity is the sister of talent.'

Anton Chekhov

Key concept

The only way to become a better writer is to sit down and do it! An important aspect of thinking like a writer is to appreciate that the process itself is the best teacher. Having a head full of rules is no substitute for grounding them in experience. The writer's perpetual challenge is to organise ideas generated by the imagination and translate them into words on the page – and it is a challenge that in a very real sense never gets easier, but surely becomes ever richer and more fulfilling.

Learning benefits

- **Sharpens an awareness of the fact that effort is closely linked to achievement (but that personal achievement is not necessarily the same as externally judged attainment or success).**
- **Cultivates an attitude of writing for the love of it.**
- **Deepens an understanding that the act of trying to frame thoughts in words brings positive benefits to many areas of life.**
- **Sharpens the wits and refines the sensibilities.**
- **Empowers us to use language more elegantly and powerfully.**

Putting pen to paper is the nitty-gritty of writing as far as most of us are concerned. All the thinking and planning come to nothing if we are not prepared to engage brain with pen and paper (or keyboard and screen). The physical act of writing is hard work, not least because of the intense concentration involved. That effort is often compounded by the frustration that can crop up quite frequently if the words just don't want to come or the whole piece of work seems to be going wrong. I think it's important for children to realise that these struggles are part of the writing process and that sticking with it is largely what brings satisfaction and a feeling of earned achievement in the end. That said, we can appreciate the comment attributed to the American writer Dorothy Parker that while she hated writing, she loved to have written.

Activities

1. Tips for writing

You might involve the class in this and include pieces of advice from the children themselves. In terms of the 'physicality' of writing attention might be paid to the following –

- Is the environment conducive to writing? Is the room warm enough and light enough?

- Are the chairs suitable and at the right height for the children to work at without discomfort? These are no petty considerations. Key 'writing and ergonomics' into your search engine and you'll see how much work has been done on this.

- Do the children have all the equipment they're likely to need in easy reach (i.e. without causing distraction by having to get up and fetch something)?

- Are children allowed 'brain breaks' during writing? What form would these take?

I feel it's worth talking with the class about this as different children will probably have different needs when it comes to freshening up their thinking. I tend to go and make a cup of tea or, if I'm writing on into the afternoon and growing tired, break off to play a video game (now that might make for an interesting classroom discussion!). Great emphasis seems to be placed on children staying 'on task' (loathsome term), but constant application can lead to weariness and boredom.

- What does a child do when she's finished his piece of work? Do you think it's best for her/him to try and edit/improve it immediately or (my preference) let it 'cool off' for a while so that she comes to it with fresh eyes later?

- What other aspects of the environment might support the effort you want the children to put into their work?

2. **Crafting the language**

Another important tips list could focus on dos and don'ts when it comes to crafting the language – although this could be something of a minefield given that we have to cultivate children's love of writing and try and move them up the levels as required by the government. As I write this I'm also mindful of Somerset Maugham's advice that there are three golden rules for writing well, and nobody knows what they are. That said, many authors (I think rightly) advocate the following –

- Have something to say. This is an obvious point to make, but it amounts to more than just reacting to a title on the board or a picture stimulus or whatever. The advice incorporates the thinking/planning techniques we've already looked at plus a certain desire and imperative in the children to want to say something. That desire is itself an amalgam of pleasure in writing for its own sake, a 'can do confidence' based on the ethos and techniques we've explored, and an increasing feeling in each child that she has her own 'take' on the subject, and that this will be valued. This final point relates to an author's 'voice' which we look at on page 104.

- Experienced writers often advise clarity, brevity, simplicity and sincerity. While we might encourage children to choose strong verbs, punchy adjectives and to use the thesaurus we would expect them to grow out of the phase of using unusual words and a range of sentence structures just because they should be able to at that age. More mature writing sets out to communicate something and gets on with it. As Matthew Arnold said 'Have something to say, and say it as clearly as you can…' This echoes advice offered long before by Hippocrates when he said 'The chief virtue that language can have is clarity.'

- George Orwell advocated five rules for effective writing. These are –

  a. Never use a metaphor, simile or other figure of speech which you are used to seeing in speech.

Following this advice is probably more difficult for older children and for adults. Younger writers enjoy the freedom of the 'beginner's mind' and won't have come across such a range of metaphors. At the very least it would be worth talking with the class about overused words and cliché, and revisiting the idea of not snatching at the first thought that comes to mind.

Zen wisdom tells us that 'In the beginner's mind there are many possibilities, while in the expert's mind there are few.' (discuss).

b. Never use a long word where a short one will do.

c. If it is possible to cut a word out, always cut it out (more on this in the next chapter Editing and improving, page 101).

d. Try to use the active voice rather than the passive voice.

e. Never use a foreign phrase, a scientific word, or a jargon word if you can think of an everyday English equivalent.

While this rule is congruent with the guidance to be clear and simple children might become confused if they are expected to use technical terms in different subject areas. What I read from Orwell here is to avoid jargon etc which can not only make writing look pretentious but adds to the difficulty of understanding it.

f. Interestingly Orwell appended a sixth rule to his list which is to avoid any of the above rules rather than saying anything 'outright barbarous'. This brings us nicely back to Basho's remark – page 16.

A classic work on clear writing is *The Elements of Style* by William Strunk and E. B. White (of *Charlotte's Web* and *Stuart Little* fame). Another book that I recommend highly is John Humphrys' *Lost For Words*.

3. On making mistakes

I wonder if like me you are still haunted by memories of having your writing book handed back only to find a story or essay littered with red-pen corrections (or worse – and surely something outright barbarous – a line through it with the admonition writ large to 'Do it again!')?

In adhering to the principles that in writing nothing is ever wasted and that practice makes better, our own and the children's attitude to making mistakes is vital. In the same way that asking questions is a sign not of stupidity but of intelligence ('I want to learn more'), so reflecting on mistakes is an opportunity to improve rather than a reason to belittle our achievement.

For me there is a world of difference between thinking 'I've done it wrong' and 'I haven't got it right yet'. An important distinction must also be drawn between 'I don't fully understand' and emergent understanding. We have all probably taught a lesson on, say, apostrophes only for our young writers to hand in work positively measled with them. While most will likely be wrongly placed, their appearance more importantly suggests that the writer is striving towards using them properly.

So in cultivating a helpful and positive attitude towards mistakes, consider incorporating some of these suggestions into your classroom practice –

● Emphasise to the children that making mistakes (when you have tried to do it well rather than because you can't be bothered) is an opportunity to improve.

- Encourage children to look back over their work and ask 'What changes can I make so that this is the best I can do?'. Also, 'What have I learned by writing this that will make my next piece even better?'.

Consider adding to your repertoire of marking symbols to reflect the 'thinking behind the writing'. A reinforcement of the fact that you value the children's thinking will help to offset any disappointment they feel when you point out mistakes and inaccuracies in their work.

8
Editing and improving

Some top tips for editing

'Art is never finished, only abandoned.'

Leonardo da Vinci (1452–1519) Italian Renaissance polymath: painter, sculptor, architect, musician, scientist, mathematician, engineer, inventor, anatomist, geologist, cartographer, botanist, and writer

---

Key concept

Looking back over a piece of work with a critical eye is a vital phase of the writing process. As teachers we guide and advise young writers on improving what they do, but surely with the aim in mind of encouraging them to become more independent in their assessment.

Learning benefits

- **Highlights the importance of the editing stage.**
- **Adds 'critical reading' to the repertoire of children's thinking skills.**
- **Develops independence of judgement.**
- **Cultivates pride in achievement when a young writer has truly tried to do his/her best.**

Activities

1. A critical eye

Sometimes work can be improved by paying close attention to the way a sentence or paragraph causes us to imagine a scene. When writing, we may suffer from 'visualisation failures', which are reflected in the language we use. Or it might work the other way round; that oddly or clumsily structured sentences cause the reader to imagine something other than what was intended.

Ask the class to pick out what's wrong with the following examples in the way they influence what we imagine. How could they be rewritten to have the intended effect?

- Running into the room, he threw open the window as he switched on the light.
- As a woman, Ben thought that she was incredibly beautiful.

- Williams saw the chaos in the street below and rubbed his nose, wondering what it would sound like.
- Like Susanna, John had dark brown hair, with enormous eyebrows, a fine moustache and handsome beard.
- Her eyes twinkled, fluttered, met his, dropped to the floor then went back to the jewels. He picked them up, held them for a moment then returned them to her with a smile.

2. Ambiguous sentences

The meaning of a sentence can be unclear for a number of reasons, such as a failure to visualise when writing. Sometimes a chosen word can have more than one meaning or the positioning of words in a sentence can cause confusion. On occasion grammatically accurate sentences simply convey insufficient information so that they can be read in more than one way (Did you spot the ambiguity in that sentence, by the way?). Ask children to notice what causes the ambiguity in these sentences and how they could be made clearer –

- Local Nurse Helps Dog Bite Victim. (Newspaper headline)
- Slow children at play.
- 'I once shot an elephant in my pyjamas.'
- Children hate annoying teachers.
- Put the book on the table in the kitchen.
- Eye drops on top shelf.
- Hospital is sued by seven foot doctors.
- Red tape holds up new bridge.
- Old playground equipment is replaced by headmaster.
- Children make nourishing snacks at school.

3. The importance of punctuation

It's important for children to realise that punctuation aids accuracy and clarity in writing. Some professional writers feel strongly that children should not be pressured into 'trying to get it right' as they write, in other words that the creative flow of language should not be interrupted by wondering where, for instance, to put an apostrophe. This is something I agree with, although I think that from the outset young writers need to understand that punctuation influences meaning, sometimes profoundly.

Show the class these examples to illustrate the point (no pun intended) –

- He chose a paperback from one of his father's bookcases./He chose a paperback from one of his fathers' bookcases.
- These two trees are my parents./These two trees are my parents'.
- Woman, without her man, is a savage./Woman: without her, man is a savage.

4. Typos

I couldn't resist including some of these, just to illustrate what a drastic effect a single letter incorrectly typed or omitted can have…

- 'Under current circumstances we see now justification for having a referendum.' (The w in 'now' is the error and gives the sentence a meaning that is completely opposite to the one that was intended.)
- 'Last night the chairman of the council let out one or two interesting farts about the new town development.' (I'm sure I don't need to explain this one, which appeared some time ago in a local newspaper.)
- After the foul was called in the twenty-eighth minute Hitchman lay writing in agony on the field.
- The golfer was his usual fashionable self and sported a stylish white car on his head.
- The mechanic was off work for six days after he dropped a wench on his foot.

5. Editing tips

The word 'edit' comes from the Latin edere 'to bring forth' and 'publish'. It's worth explaining to the children that in editing their work –

- They are preparing it to be 'made public', bringing it forth in the sense that the effort at this stage is to make the work the best it can be.
- If they have thought about what they wanted to say, chosen their words carefully, checked for sense, accuracy and their highest standards of presentation then they can enjoy a sense of achievement for having done their best.
- Reinforce the fact that writers never stop learning: there is always potential for improvement.
- Cultivate the attitude that nothing is ever wasted. Mistakes have learning value if children are prepared to consider them in that way. Every word written is a step on the road to further improvement.

Some further tips you might offer to the class are –

- Don't try to correct work as you write it. If the words are not flowing as you want them to, or if you feel you've made a mistake, think, check and edit later. What's important is that you get your thoughts down even if they seem a bit muddled at the moment. Make a note to come back to particular points, but don't let that interrupt the writing itself.
- After finishing a first draft, put it away for a while to 'cool off'. Look at it later with fresh eyes.
- When you do go back to your writing, if you want to change something just put a line through it rather than scribbling over it. That way, afterwards you'll be able to see how your mind worked as you set about improving your work.

Teacher tip

You can formalise the editing process by advising children to rule a line down the middle of their writing paper. Ask them to write their piece on one side and afterwards annotate their work with a critical eye on the other side. See the section 'Some practice' below for an example.

Consider displaying these points prominently so the children are constantly reminded of them:

- Let others read your work. Be proud of your achievement. Listen to advice and consider it – you don't have to agree with it (but if you don't have at least one reason why not).

- Also, if anyone points out errors or ways you can improve don't take it as a personal criticism. All determined writers are trying to improve – we're all in the same boat.

- By the same token if you are asked to comment on someone else's work, be respectful of the writer's feelings.

- Apply the 3–1 rule. When you look at your work, for every one thing you think you can improve, find three things you feel you've done well.

- Don't pick at your work endlessly. Look through it a couple of times, make corrections and then leave it for the next project. You can ask yourself, 'What have I learned by writing and editing this that could make my next piece of writing better?'

Some practice

'Have been correcting the proofs of my poems. In the morning, after hard work, I took a comma out of one sentence… In the afternoon I put it back again.'

Oscar Wilde (1854–1900) Irish writer and poet

Key concepts

Editing (or 'looking back' as I prefer to call it) adds a new set of skills to the craft of writing. I advise children to leave the 'tweaking' until they've written the first draft: trying to create and correct simultaneously is difficult and can prevent young writers from 'getting into' the work. Important aspects of editing include looking for logical inconsistencies and deciding if the words that were chosen initially are the most effective. These two elements form the focus of the practice piece below.

Background: The opening scenes of Silent victim (see below) were written by 16-year-old Bita. English is not her first language and she had been learning it for only a few years when she wrote the story. Bita's ambition is to become a professional writer.

Show the class the extract and ask the children to notice how they visualise the scene. On looking back over her writing Bita noticed several things that she could change to improve the work (see below).

Silent victim

Nothing ever happened in Northwick. It was that sort of village; predictable. A place you passed through en route to somewhere more enticing without any registering its existence. Even their church, in a county famous for its churches, was dull and uninteresting, and attracted a few visitors.

After months of drought the storm, when it came, was a welcome relief. The heavy droplets bounced off the red, slatted roofs and gushed along the drains and gutters, dragging with them the soot and dirt which had built up from the summer months, before finally spilling out on the roads and pavements and reflecting the street lamps in pools of shimmering light.

PC Jay Morris stood impassively under an ancient yew whose branches stretched out over the cemetery wall, offering him a temporary sanctuary from the restless downpour. As he watched the water drip from the tip of his helmet, the church clock struck the quarter hour. He looked down at his watch; one forty-five. There was just enough time to check the last few shops on the high street before making his way back to the station to dry out and investigate the mysteries of his sandwich box.

Despite, working shifts for almost twenty five years PC Jay still hated nights, there was something unnatural about them. Nights were meant for warm beds, not hard roads and wet feet. As the lightning forked across the sky and the thunder rolled over head, he pulled the collar of his raincoat tightly around his neck, secured his helmet strap and left his leafy refuge.

Energy Mark James had left in his body was knocked out by the fall. He lay on his back, peering through the rain, letting it splash over his face and along his lips, taking in deep gulps of air, his ribcage rising and falling with each rasping breath. Fear had dried his mouth and was suddenly very thirsty. He licked his lips, picking up the droplets from the end of his throat, providing momentarily relief. He needed time, time to think, time to sort out what had happened, everything had gone so well. How had he been found out so quickly? He wondered now whether he had made a grave error in crossing Bird for a second time. He normally knew when to quit, but this time seemed to have made a big mistake, gone too far, and now was running for his very life.

He had left no sense of apprehension when the car had arrived. It had followed the agreed procedures to the letter. Stopped, flashed its light twice quickly and then once slowly, just as arranged. The only thing he had found a little unusual was the location. He was a bit of a moth and liked to hover around the bright lights of the city.

Despite living in Cambridge all his life he'd never heard of Northwick. It was a cold, isolated place in the middle of nowhere, the kind of village which people came to retire and die. He hoped he'd never see it again. Still, the man must have had his reasons, and whatever they were it was fine by him.

Silent Victim

Maybe a stronger beginning if I said 'Nothing ever happened in Northwick – but that was about to change. Usually it was a predictable sort of village…' Who does 'their' refer to? Change to 'the'.	Nothing ever happened in Northwick. It was that sort of village; predictable. A place you passed through en route to somewhere more enticing without any registering its existence. Even their church, in a county famous for its churches, was dull and uninteresting, and attracted a few visitors.
Change to 'gutters and drains', since the water will reach the gutters first. Does soot build up on roofs? Would you have soot around anyway in the summer?	After months of drought the storm, when it came, was a welcome relief. The heavy droplets bounced off the red, slatted roofs and gushed along the drains and gutters, dragging with them the soot and dirt which had built up from the summer months, before finally spilling out on the roads and pavements and reflecting the street lamps in pools of shimmering light.
Does a police helmet have a tip? Could I say 'brim'? Must check. The church clock wouldn't strike the quarter hour at 1.45. Could change to 'the church clock sounded (or chimed?); Morris checked his watch, one forty-five'. Would a village have a policeman on night shift? Maybe. Northwick must be quite big if there are a number of shops on the high street.	PC Jay Morris stood impassively under an ancient yew whose branches stretched out over the cemetery wall, offering him a temporary sanctuary from the restless downpour. As he watched the water drip from the tip of his helmet, the church clock struck the quarter hour. He looked down at his watch; one forty-five. There was just enough time to check the last few shops on the high street before making his way back to the station to dry out and investigate the mysteries of his sandwich box.

No need to say PC again as we already know his job. Would a night shift end at 2.00 a.m.? Hmm – what do I intend to mean by saying there was something 'unnatural' about nights?	Despite, working shifts for almost twenty five years PC Jay still hated nights, there was something unnatural about them. Nights were meant for warm beds, not hard roads and wet feet. As the lightning forked across the sky and the thunder rolled over head, he pulled the collar of his raincoat tightly around his neck, secured his helmet strap and left his leafy refuge.
'Leafy' refuge? Checked that and they are called leaves on a yew. But the word does give the impression of trees like maple or chestnut.	
I think I prefer 'Any energy that Mark James had left in his body was knocked out of him by the fall.'	Energy Mark James had left in his body was knocked out by the fall. He lay on his back, peering through the rain, letting it splash over his face and along his lips, taking in deep gulps of air, his ribcage rising and falling with each rasping breath. Fear had dried his mouth and was suddenly very thirsty. He licked his lips, picking up the droplets from the end of his throat, providing momentarily relief. He needed time, time to think, time to sort out what had happened, everything had gone so well. How had he been found out so quickly? He wondered now whether he had made a grave error in crossing Bird for a second time. He normally knew when to quit, but this time seemed to have made a big mistake, gone too far, and now was running for his very life.
Did he fall on to his back, or did he fall forwards then turn over?	
'and he was suddenly very thirsty'.	
'the end of his throat' sounds odd. Prefer 'He licked his lips, the moisture on them providing momentary relief.'	
(I'm pleased with this part; it makes the reader wonder what James has done.)	
Does 'running for his life' sound right when he's lying on his back?	
'It' means the car. Sounds better to say 'The driver'. Change 'he' to 'James'.	He had no sense of apprehension when the car had arrived. It had followed the agreed procedures to the letter. Stopped, flashed its light twice quickly and then once slowly, just as arranged. The only thing he had found a little unusual was the location. He was a bit of a moth and liked to hover around the bright lights of the city.
'where people came…' Prefer 'Still, Bird must have had his reasons…'	Despite living in Cambridge all his life he'd never heard of Northwick. It was a cold, isolated place in the middle of nowhere, the kind of village which people came to retire and die. He hoped he'd never see it again. Still, the man must have had his reasons, and whatever they were it was fine by him.

Finding your voice

'Don't expect anything original from an echo.'

Author unknown

Key concept

All the effort and determination that writers put into their craft leads toward the establishment of that author's individual voice. Experienced writers not only communicate clearly, but do so with a distinctive style that marks it out as their work.

Activities

1. Finding a voice

Many aspects of writing contribute to what I'm calling the author's voice; not just stylistic techniques but the forms, genres and themes that an author favours. The concept is subtle and sophisticated and sometimes difficult for children to understand. A useful activity is to say to the class 'If I read you a few pages of a Harry Potter story, how would you know it's Harry Potter?' Prompt the children to look beyond the obvious aspects such as character names, distinctive terms such as quidditch, etc. Now probe further with questions such as…

- What do you like about the way your favourite author writes?
- How does this author make characters, places and events believable?
- Do you think the stories by your favourite author 'tell you something true'? (see page 63). If so, what do you learn? If you read just to 'visit that world', what makes that place so interesting and convincing?
- What themes does that author like to explore? Are any of these themes important in your life?
- If you could change any aspect of the way your favourite author writes, what would it be?
- If your favourite author asked you to write his/her next novel, short story, poem etc what would it be about?
- If you could ask your author three questions what would they be (and why did you choose these particular questions?)

(Suitable for Key Stage 1)

2. Towards originality

The poet and educational writer Pie Corbett feels that we develop as writers through the phases of imitation, innovation and invention. We begin by deliberately mimicking the style, genre and themes of authors we admire. Since this is a natural (and probably an inevitable) part of a young writer's apprenticeship it is not only to be accepted but encouraged. Similarly writers starting out who favour a particular genre are likely at first to explore 'well trodden ground' and produce ideas that are obvious or old hat. Again this is to be expected as a necessary part of learning the craft: educationally what matters is that the child is writing for pleasure.

This last point touches on the notion of originality. It is often assumed I think that original ideas somehow suddenly appear out of the blue and that they are, or should be, original in the general sense of never having been thought of by anyone before. This is not only an unrealistic expectation but shows a lack of understanding about how the creative process works. An original thought amounts to a new connection between two or more previously unrelated ideas. When children actively write for enjoyment ('actively' in the sense that they desire to learn more about the craft) the groundwork is being laid that will eventually lead to the emergence of their own individual voice and a fresh perception of the material with which they are working. As a precursor to the production of truly original work, young writers will be making many connections that are new to them, even if their ideas are unoriginal in the general sense; i.e. many people have had them before.

Innovation (from the Latin 'to renew or change') marks an important step towards the establishment of a writer's unique voice and – hopefully – her expression of original ideas. Innovation strictly means the use of a new idea or method rather than the creation of new ideas or methods (i.e. their invention). It might be usefully seen as a halfway house between reliance on the way other writers work and the appearance of more independent thinking and a fresher exploration of themes/genres and forms.

Innovation is not something that can be forced or taught, in so far as its emergence lies at the heart of a child's attitude towards the craft. However a classroom environment that allows regular writing time (for pleasure), that celebrates every child's efforts, that guides and encourages young writers to explore and experiment; and an ethos promoting the notion that effort plus enjoyment equals achievement will do much to help children realise their potential as writers.

3. Collaboration

Some children might prefer working with a partner rather than forging on alone. Certainly in the early stages of generating ideas, talking things through with a friend or brainstorming ideas as part of a group can produce more and better ideas than working individually. But having a 'writing buddy' is also useful throughout the writing process. Here are some techniques for collaborative writing.

- Parallel writing. Two young writers develop a plot and characters together, then each writes his own version of the story. Subsequent discussion 'unpacks' the way that each writer has tackled the subject, looking at differences and similarities of approach and wording, etc and articulating reasons why each writer did things in that particular way.

- Handing on the baton. Having planned a story (or other kind of writing) one partner makes a start and agrees to write for a certain time. After that time, even if he's in mid-sentence, the writer hands over to his partner to carry on. The work proceeds turn-and-turn-about, then both writers look over the first draft to discuss ways of improving the work.

- Ping-pong tales. This idea is a variation of 'handing on the baton'. Writing partners plan a piece of work and ping-pong it backwards and forwards until it's finished. Each writer can then independently suggest ways of improving the work, leading to a joint discussion that incorporates the most useful ideas. The technique can be taken further by having two pieces of writing on the go at once.

- Critical friend. The writing buddy role might prove more useful at the editing stage, where the emphasis of the collaboration is not in creating the piece of work but reflecting on it once a child has finished the first draft. Supportive suggestions for improving the writing might be done 'annotated notebook style' (see Silent Victim on page 105) or simply by talking the piece through together. This arrangement accommodates children who prefer to work alone but who nevertheless would benefit from constructive feedback.

- Writing tutor. An extension of the critical friend idea is to have a more experienced and confident young writer tutor another child, perhaps from a different class or year group. There would need to be a mutual understanding that both writers 'are on the same road together' – i.e. both learning and developing, connected by a common love of the craft. There should be no suggestion that the tutor is a 'better' writer than the person he is helping (even if the child being tutored believes that). The value of this technique is that the tutor role is distinct from that of the teacher, who necessarily must be corrective in approach, compare a child's work with other children's writing and judge it against agreed criteria.

- Five-minute expert. These events can be set up very easily and take the form of a brief 'teach me how' talk. So a child who loves writing action stories might offer the audience some tips on how he does that, while another young writer might offer insights on creating haiku, etc. These short talks combine a few examples with some practical advice, though all are linked by a common enthusiasm for the subject.

'Think what is going to make your story sing in the readers' mind. Then they are going to listen to you.'

Alan Gibbons

Celebrate writing

'Not knowing when the dawn will come, I open every door.'

Emily Dickinson (1830–1886) American poet

Key concept

Writing for pleasure is an idea that attracts most children when it is built into the ethos of the whole school. Part of the pleasure comes from the understanding that writing effectively makes us more powerful communicators. As such we can express ourselves more fluently, understand concepts more readily, enjoy reading as a richer experience and become more creative, independent and self-confident thinkers. These developing abilities bring benefits across the whole of a child's school life and beyond.

Whole-school projects

As a way of celebrating a love of writing for its own sake (though with all of the attendant advantages in mind), consider organising whole-school projects. Here are some that I've come across in my travels…

- Ask the panel. Occasionally, perhaps during assembly time, invite some children (and staff?) who love writing to sit on a panel and take questions from the audience. These might be of the 'what do you like to write' variety but could just as easily address practical problems that other children might encounter in their work.

- Agony aunt. Here the emphasis is on sharing advice. One way of running this is to set up a display board where young writers post questions and others (again including staff) suggest solutions. Postings can be anonymous if preferred.

- Quotes board. Make a colourful display of quotes about writing from children, staff, parents, well-known writers etc. Related ideas are –
  - Top tips for better writing.
  - Brief book reviews.
  - Fascinating facts about famous writers.
  - Workshop suggestions.

- Letters to writers. Many schools already do this. Contact details for writers can often be found on their own or publishers' websites. Or letters can be sent c/o the publisher. Impress on children that many writers (especially the more successful ones) are very busy and replies to the letters might be a long time in coming or might not appear at all. If you do want to encourage children to write to a popular author, I suggest one letter from the whole class is appropriate if it contains questions – although multiple letters saying how much children have enjoyed a writer's work are usually appreciated.

- Story trails. A different class or group should be responsible for arranging a story trail each time, perhaps on a half-termly basis. The idea is to place a number of pictures/objects around the school and inviting others to link them in a story. A map of where the items are and in which order they need to be visited (if that matters) can prove useful. Finished stories can be displayed, read out or told at special storytelling events etc. The selection of story trail objects as well as well as completed stories can form the basis for the creation of board games (see page 86).

- Round robin. A number of children sign up to be 'round robineers', agreeing to devote at least 15 minutes to thinking/writing each time a story comes their way. Put a story starter on the first page of an exercise book or folder and pass to the first round robineer, who then adds to the tale before passing it on. The order in which children receive the story can be determined by alphabetical order of surname, first come first served, drawing names from a bag etc. Round robin stories can circulate within a class, a year, or the whole school. Some children might prefer to draw their extract. More than one round robin story book can be circulating at any given time.

- Story time. Reading, telling and performing stories (and poems) can be justified educationally in many ways. Indeed it would surely need to be a clever argument to convince us that 'story time' did not have huge learning value. Story time ideally should not just be a filler if there is nothing else that needs to be done, but integral to the structure of the school day. Involving the children in terms of telling stories themselves adds variety and interest. Tellings might be prepared beforehand, or be a more informal and conversational swapping of anecdotes.

- Presentations to the class, the whole school and to parents and other invited guests form a natural extension to the activities above. They need not be elaborate (on the scale of a school play or panto for instance) but again should be staged on a regular basis. To bring variety to the presentations children might offer readings of their work, dramatisations, slide shows, displays of linked artwork and so on. In more than one school I've visited a presentation event has been run during a parents' evening or school open day. On such occasions the children involved are often pride personified (as are their parents)!

- School publication. Some schools celebrate writing by producing a regular writing newsletter, magazine or even – more ambitiously – a professionally published anthology of work. The immediate value is to the children who enjoy the thrill of seeing their work in print, but such projects also reflect positively on the school as a whole and can generate some great local publicity. Modest publications might be printed 'in-house', though if as a school you decide to invest in a more polished magazine or book many printing and self-publishing companies offer a professional service.

- Writing club. It's likely that in every school there are several children who aspire to be published authors or otherwise base a career on some aspect of writing (such as journalism). Young writers like these often want to devote more time to the craft, and work at it more intensively, than can be accommodated in the classroom on a day-to-day basis. A writing club is logistically easy to organise and is an effective way of serving their needs. Children who come regularly and 'stay the course' are also likely to be quite independent and self-determining – usually they know what they want to write and just get on with it. (As a personal aside the writing club I ran at school was a haven of peace and what I can only call 'contented concentration'. I wrote along with the children. Occasionally one might come up to my desk and ask for a piece of advice – sometimes I made a point of asking one of them for the same! – but most times we just enjoyed the feeling of sitting there in good company, joined by the act of doing something we all loved.)

Last words

'It's not what you look at that matters, it's what you see.'

Henry David Thoreau (1817–1862) American author, poet and philosopher

When a child thinks like a writer she is looking at the world through both a creative and a critical eye. She is actively generating deeper and more sophisticated meanings out of what she encounters. She enjoys experiencing the world with what the educationalist Margaret Meek has called a sense of 'firstness': the world itself seems fresh and original because that's how the child's mind engages with it. And yet such an awareness is not naïve or gullible. Increasingly a young writer, relishing the ongoing adventure of translating experiences into words, becomes more shrewdly informed about language and, I believe, less likely to be manipulated by what others write and say.

The challenge of 'walking the good road' explored in this book increases the chances of turning a writer into an author. I don't necessarily mean becoming a published author – though when talent, enthusiasm and opportunity meet for a child the chances of that outcome are greatly increased. When I speak to children about 'being an author' I ask them to imagine that word then add '-ity' at the end. They tell me then with a dawning realisation that an authority is someone who is in control, who has influence, who makes up his own mind and retains the power to determine. But perhaps even more importantly a child who thinks like a writer (or author) enjoys a richer life both in the 'real world' and in the equally valuable realm of the imagination. As Ellie (Year 4) once told me –

'You know it's good when you're inside the story, all of you is in there and you are nowhere else in the world.'

Bibliography

Bowkett, S. (2004) *If I Were a Spider*, Stafford: Network Educational Press

Bowkett, S. (2007) *100+ Ideas for Teaching Thinking Skills*, London: Continuum

Bowkett, S. (2009) *Countdown to Poetry Writing*, London: Routledge

Bowkett, S. (2009) *Countdown to Non-Fiction Writing*, London: Routledge

Bowkett, S. (2010) *Developing Literacy and Creative Writing Through Storymaking: story strands for 7–12 year-olds*, Maidenhead: Open University Press

Bowkett, S. & Percival, S. (2011) *Coaching Emotional Intelligence in the Classroom*, London: Routledge

Brownjohn, S. (1980) *Does It Have to Rhyme?*, London: Hodder Education

Dweck, C. (2000) *Self-Theories: their role in motivation, personality and development*, New York: Psychology Press

Egan, K. (1989) *Teaching As Story Telling*, Chicago: University of Chicago Press

Gardner, W.H. (1970) *Gerard Manley Hopkins: poems and prose*, Harmondsworth: Penguin

Hughes, T. (2008) *Poetry in the Making*, London: Faber & Faber

Humphreys, J. (2004) *Lost for Words*, London: Hodder & Stoughton

Longman Dictionary of Word Origins (1983) Harlow, Essex

Morgan, N. & Saxton, J. (2002) *Asking Better Questions* Markham, Ontario: Pembroke Publishers

O'Connor J. & Seymour, J. (2003) *Introducing Neuro-Linguistic Programming*, London: Thorsons

Rockett, M. & Percival, S. (2002) *Thinking for Learning* Stafford, Network Educational Press

Rowland, M. (2005) *The Philosopher at the End of the Universe*, London: Ebury Press

Sedgwick, F. (2010) *100 ideas for Teaching Poetry*, London: Continuum

Strunk, W. & White, E. B. (1999)*The Elements of Style*, New York: Longman

Tilling, M. (2001) *Adventures in Learning*, Stafford: Network Educational Press

van den Brink-Budgen, R. (2010) *Critical Thinking for Students*, Oxford: How To Books

Voytilla, S. (1999) *Myth and The Movies*, Studio City CA: Michael Weise Productions

A Creative Approach to
Teaching Writing